Being God's

BeGods!
Jimmy Cocina
2008

Being God's

A Single Guy's Walk With God

Jimmy Cochran

Library of Congress Control Number:		2006910395
ISBN 10:	Hardcover	1-4257-4550-4
	Softcover	1-4257-4549-0
ISBN 13:	Hardcover	978-1-4257-4550-9
	Softcover	978-1-4257-4549-3

This book was printed in the United States of America.

To order additional copies of this book, contact:
Xlibris Corporation
1-888-795-4274
www.Xlibris.com
Orders@Xlibris.com
33035

Contents

Acknowledgements 9
Introduction 11

WATCHING AS THE WORLD PASSES

The Venusian finally Reaches Adulthood 15
The Day I Went Back to School 17
Funyaking with God 19
I Broke One of My Rules Today 21
What a Day! 23
Refuge From The Storm 25
Being Icebound with a Neurotic Single Guy 27
People of Vision 29
The Thugs Meet the Geezers 31
From the Mouth of a Child 33
Diversity in Aqua-World 35
"Hey, Mr. Jimmy. This is Tonya." 37

JUST ME AND GOD

Thinking Back, Looking Forward 41
Beware the Barberry 43
Don't Worry! Be God's! 45
Late Night Musings 47
Perspective and Blessings 48
Shhhh! God Is Trying To Talk! 50
The Curse of the Cowlick 52
When the War Hits Home 54
Transparencies and Masquerades 56
The Intruder 58

FAMILY, FRIENDS AND GENERAL DYSFUNCTION

No, I Do Not Dye My Hair!! 63
Go Ye Therefore—by Instant Messenger, Blogs and Text Messages 65
The Eyes of the Man 67
Dads! Gotta Love 'Em! 69
The Great Equalizer 71
And It Continues 73
The Waiting is Hell 74
Free at Last! 76

LIFE THROUGH A SINGLE GUY'S EYES

The Journey of Living Single 79
A Dreaded Thing Appeared In My Mailbox 81
In the Sanctuary of my SUV 83
Well, Here We Go Again! 84
Looking Back, Looking Forward 86
Me and My Luggage 87
Murphy's Law—(a tongue in cheek story, but, sadly true) 89
Lessons Learned from My Dog 91
Biting the Hand that Feeds You 93
The Rock and a Hard Place 95
A Day of Loss 96
The Hound Of Heaven 98
My House Speaks 100
Valentine's Day and the Single Guy 102
Why Not Me? 103
What Does Your Coffee Table Say? 105
Being a Man of God 107
Afterword 109

With all the love in my heart, I dedicate this book to my mother, my sister and my brother. I offer a special dedication to my father who did not live to see the completion of this work, but I know he would be proud of what I have accomplished.

Acknowledgements

In a book like this, it is difficult to thank all those who need thanking. Pastors, teachers, musicians, family, friends, neighbors, animals and even those strange people you see wandering around in the mall have all played a part in my writing. However, a few people have proved to be most encouraging to me as a writer and to put these articles into book form.

The Single Adults of Salem Baptist Church in McDonough, Georgia—thank you for supporting and encouraging me from the very beginning. Your emails, phone calls and words as we are together keep me going and constantly challenge me to think about how to speak to the single adult population.

Shannon Woodward—You have been both a mentor and friend to me in the blogging world and as I began to consider the possibility of putting my writing into book form. Thank you for your love for our Lord and for your help and encouragement to me. I also appreciate your honest critiques and copyediting of this book.

Victoria Gaines—You introduced me to the Christian writing possibilities and held me accountable for always being truthful and honest. Thank you for giving me the impetus to see God's plan for me in writing.

Fay Jacobs and Marc Acito—Even though we have never met face to face, you have both been an encouragement by your willingness to see the lessons in everyday life and the realistic style of your writing. Our emails back and forth have taught me much about being uncompromising as a writer, regardless of topic. Unbeknownst to me, Marc has also used the "Gospel according to Marc" tagline for as long as I have used the "Gospel according to Jimmy" tagline and I appreciate his willingness to allow me to use it in print along with him.

Fay Jacobs—("As I Lay Frying", A&M Books, May 2004)
Marc Acito—("How I Paid for College", Broadway Publishing, August 2005)

Josh Clark, Editor, and the Henry County Times newspaper staff—you gave me a start when I was a newbie in the writing world. I appreciate the advice and support you offered me as I began my biweekly column and as I grew as a writer. Unless otherwise notated, all the articles in this book were originally published in the Henry County Times and I look forward to a long relationship with the paper as I already plan for the next book.

Thank you to my friend, Gabe Walker, who wrote the introduction to this book. Even though he is afraid of clowns, he has been a faithful and true friend and I knew he could introduce this book with an insight to my intent and purpose. His dedication and love for God is an inspiration to me and to many others through his ministry.

I have been blessed with good friends and faithful readers. Without them, I would never have made it this far. Your unfailing love and gentle kicks of encouragement when I would lose my vision of this book helped me through the difficult days. I love you all.

Introduction

I once said that my life goal was to watch every movie ever made. I would start at the local Blockbuster and gradually make my way through the aisles. New releases. Old favorites. Classics. And all the ones in between.

I love movies. It doesn't matter what genre. Action. Drama. Comedy. Just give me my popcorn, turn off the lights, turn up the sound and silence everything around me for a couple of hours.

I think the reason I enjoy movies so greatly is because of a connection to the stories they tell. Stories of people's lives; their experiences, their journeys.

And I think each of us can find movies to which we relate. The power of love in "A Beautiful Mind"; the hope and salvation in "The Matrix"; the overcoming of racism and hatred in "Remember the Titans"; the influence of the past in "Eternal Sunshine of the Spotless Mind"; the feeling of triumph in "Rocky"; or society's need for a hero in "Superman".

Stories of hope and faith, love and relationships, enduring and overcoming trials, stories we can embrace and every emotion we are capable of experiencing.

Stories.

Each of us has a story. A journey of experiences, relationships, decisions and defining moments that has shaped us into who we are today. Every moment, every conversation, every experience somehow woven together into some great tapestry.

I think that is a beautiful and powerful thing.

People connect with our story. They relate to us because of our story. Our story makes us real; and perhaps that's what we crave most, to be real and to be with others who are real.

That's what I find in "Being God's". Someone who is real. Raw, unfiltered honesty in reaction to the circumstances and events within life; fully believing that his story has the power to impact others; and, that at the core of everything there is a Creator holding everything and circumstance to reveal His glory and His unfolding plan.

When I read Jimmy's story, I find a man who is completely transparent with his motives, a man who is genuine with his love and concern for others, and who has completely abandoned himself to the call of Jesus.

I find that refreshing. I don't think we see much of that anymore.

No masks.

No games.

Simply real.

What would happen if each of us felt the freedom to tell our stories?
No desire to impress.
No more worrying about what others think.
No more hiding.
No more pretending.
Completely exposed and vulnerable, each of us begins to freely share our joys, our hurts, our dreams, and our frustrations. And perhaps for the first time, we find comfort instead of judgment, restoration instead of condemnation encouragement instead of guilt. Perhaps, for the first time, we experience community. Community the way Jesus intended.
Imagine.
I believe that is what Jimmy is guiding each of us towards. A place of being real. A place where I can open my heart, tell my story and really connect with people in a way that changes lives. I want to be there, fully there.
And I believe that each of us, somewhere deep down inside, has that same desire.
And it begins with telling my story.
May you today, from deep within your heart, tell your story. It has the power to impact people at their most personal level, at the very core of their being, and it opens the door to the road of becoming real.

Gabe Walker
2006

Watching as the World Passes

The Venusian finally Reaches Adulthood

When I was a young boy in fourth grade, I wrote a short story entitled "The Venusian." It was a quite adventuresome story about a boy who discovered that a tree in his backyard had a hidden doorway that, when entered, could transport him to Venus. So, over a period of time, the boy traveled to Venus and in turn, his Venusian friends traveled to Earth. The boy and his extra-terrestrial friends had quite a number of adventures and, if I recall, there was even a sequel written at some point. Sadly to say, those manuscripts have since been lost (or perhaps taken to Venus for safekeeping) so mankind will never benefit from the adventures of "The Venusian".

My love and passion for reading and writing began that year. Through high school and college, you could always find me with my head stuck in some book reading for hours (unfortunately they weren't always my textbooks) or I was keeping a journal of some type. I always thought it so cool how John-Boy Walton and Doogie Howser both kept journals at the end of each program. For many years, I kept bound journals with handwritten entries (like John Boy) and then after I acquired technology in my house, I began using more technological methods (i.e., Doogie Howser).

Now, even as an adult, I've held onto my dream of being a writer. After watching the movie "Julia" with Vanessa Redgrave, Jason Robards and Jane Fonda, the most wonderful career for me seemed to be to have a beach house like Jane Fonda had where I could sit and type, smoke cigarettes, and finally throw the typewriter out the window with a flourish in artistic despair. Then, a few decades later, I would watch the "Dave Barry Show" and wish for a career in writing at home in my bathrobe all day. Could life be any cooler than that? However, as the days, months and years passed, I would stick to my occasional journal writing and the once in a while church newsletter article about a pot luck dinner or bowling tournament.

Then, one day a couple years ago, I began to notice how God was teaching me lessons in my daily life. Some of them involved things Murphy (my terrier) would do, some were work-related, and others involved family, friends or just ordinary life incidents. I would start to put these thoughts down on paper (well, on monitor) and before long a halfway decent devotional stared back at me. From that day on, more and more of my time became consumed with writing my thoughts and impressions down in a devotional or Christian article format and sharing them with friends in my church and in the community.

Before long, I began writing on a blog. Not to get my name out there as being anybody's big woo, but as a vehicle for my writing and possible creating some discussion.

As a result, my life has been enriched one hundred fold. I've met some of the neatest people imaginable as we post and comment back and forth, I have become a contributor for several internet magazines and am one of the religion columnists for the Henry County Times, writing articles on a regular basis. I am so extremely excited because this is what I've always dreamed of doing. Plus, I realize that God has been working toward this all these years and (being God), never let on to me what He had planned until now.

"Thank you, God, for your blessings to me and keep my heart and mind receptive to You in these coming weeks so that I can share your Love with people in a way that they might understand."

And I am certain of one other thing. That somewhere, far far away, the Venusian and the little boy are standing there clapping their hands and various Venusian appendages in excitement, too. I just wish they were here to share the honor.

And for today my friends, this has been the gospel according to Jimmy.

The Day I Went Back to School

"Jesus loves the little children; all the children of the world.
Red and yellow, black and white;
They are precious in His sight,
Jesus loves the little children of the world." (Children's song)

Recently, I had the privilege of speaking for Career Day at a local elementary school. The counselor who set up the day asked me to speak to the boys and girls in third, fourth and fifth grade classes about being a newspaper and magazine columnist and the importance of reading for fun. I also got to meet and visit with one of the very special classes of children at the school and see a theatrical production of "The Hungry Caterpillar" which received rave reviews from all who attended.

Going into the day, I was rather apprehensive because I had never done this type of thing before. Oh, I enjoy being around children and being a part of their energy and enthusiasm for life, but I had not set foot in an elementary school for quite a few years. If I recall, my elementary school will not even allow me back inside the doors because of my childhood behavior issues. My usual insecurity levels were on full alert in case I was rejected by the children and they started throwing crayons, glue and invectives at me. My imagination was already conceiving of police and SWAT teams coming into the school building to try and squash a riot of third graders because they were bored to tears from some old man talking about the importance of the ABC's and actually going inside the library for fun.

How wrong could I have been? I could not have asked for a more well-behaved group of boys and girls if I had placed an order from the Good Child catalog. And the great thing was that I do not think they behaved so well because their teachers had threatened them with bodily torture or having to write sentences on the chalkboard (what am I saying? Schools don't even have chalkboards anymore). The children behaved because I think they were interested in what I and the other visitors had to say. Plus, I think they were just good and polite boys and girls.

I was also very encouraged by the diversity of the school. There were children from many ethnic backgrounds, teachers from many ethnic backgrounds and it was good for my heart to see the acceptance, without seemingly any question about it. Folks, that's how it should be. Why can't we as adults learn from these children? Oh, I'm not so blind to think there aren't problems and issues in this school and many others, however, here is the beginning. We as the grownups just need to watch and get a clue as to how to make it happen in our worlds.

God accepts and extends His Love to all—Jew and Gentile, higher and lower income levels, all ethnic groups and cultures, mean people and nice people, men and women, rednecks and socialites, ugly people and pretty people, Americans and Europeans, and so on. All we have to do is accept the fact that He loves us and sees us as equal in His eyes. Once we come to that point, it is easier to see our neighbors and communities with the same view.

Thank you for inviting me to school for part of a day to try and share a little of what I have learned and do each day. Thank you especially for your teaching me far more about how we as adults should be living. You've caught on to the secret; I just hope that the rest of us can.

And that, my friends, is the gospel according to Jimmy.

Funyaking with God

"Trust in the Lord with all your heart and don't rely in your own understanding of things. Don't try to be as wise as you think you should be and He will direct your way in life." (Proverbs 3:5-6)

I recently spent a weekend on the river with a bunch of 11th graders from the church. Besides the river, we also camped out alongside the river on what we thought was high ground until the rains arrived about 10:30 that night. I never realized so many people could sleep in a church van and a utility trailer.

I learned a lot of life lessons in those two days. One is that I really enjoyed camping. It had been a long time since I had actually camped in a tent in a sleeping bag on the ground (as opposed to my normal camping at a rented condo or Hampton Inn). I also enjoyed camp food . . . the smell of the fire, the wonderful aroma of grilling chicken and vegetables, the fellowship you find while making s'mores, etc. Of course, I quickly remembered why you don't put your tent with the doorway facing the fire . . . . the wind is gonna eventually shift directions.

But, I was reminded of one of God's most important lessons while funyaking down the river. It wasn't a high skill level trek, but with all the recent rains, the river and rapids were a little faster than prior years. One of the primary goals when funyakking, kayaking, canoeing, rafting or tubing is to try and hit the rapids going forward because you can see your way clearer for paddling and you also expose less of your craft and your body to the rocks and the rushing water. Knowing this and doing this are two separate things, as I learned. My funyak partner and I tried our best to keep our craft straight and true, but no matter how hard we paddled, we would hit those rapids sideways and get drenched and almost tossed out. However, as we began to get our rhythms of paddling together and correctly, we were able to keep straight and flow through the turbulence with less turmoil.

Do you see where I'm going? Probably not, so here is what I learned or at least remembered. When we hit the storms and trials of life head on with our paddles in rhythm with God, then we can come through with less mess than when our lives are out of rhythm with Him. We still get wet and tossed, but with God as our partner, we will come through. When we try to do our own thing and leave God on the shore is when we are buffeted and drenched and thrown from our comfort places. Sometimes we survive, sometimes we don't. Sometimes we just have to ride home in a van full of wet soggy teenagers who smell like feet.

We all hit the rapids and waterfalls of life. It is inevitable. It may be a divorce, a death in the family, stress on the job, a job loss, and physical or emotional illnesses, whatever. Trust God even when you don't feel His presence in your life. He is always there waiting for you to trust Him with your rapids and waterfalls. Just don't forget to thank Him when you hit the smooth waters.

And for today my friends, this has been the gospel according to Jimmy.

I Broke One of My Rules Today

"Do not neglect to show hospitality to strangers, for by this some have entertained angels without knowing it." (Hebrews 13:2)

I broke one of my cardinal rules today and the scary part is that I don't even feel guilty about it. You see, I have worked in downtown Atlanta for quite a few years and it is almost impossible to leave any building without being approached by one of the "urban dwellers" (i.e., homeless, drifters, beggars, etc). Well, in my most humanistic mind I try to avoid these people at all costs using one or more of the below methods:

1) avoid eye contact
2) cross to the other side of the sidewalk or street
3) talk to any other human being about the weather or something until you get past them
4) put Ipod® headhones in my ears so I can avoid hearing anything
5) pretend to not speak English

As a side note, our Bible Study this quarter at church has been on angels and as another coincidence, the above scripture was part of a study this past week for one of my school classes. I think that God was just setting me up to teach me a lesson . . . . and was probably quite amused by it.

Now, back to today. I was leaving for the day and a man approached me (no iPod® available, in a hallway with no escape) and asked me the time. I gave it to him and then he asked me if I had any friends of his particular ethnic background. I answered 'yes' (while continuing to walk) and he said his car had been towed and he needed transit fare to the impound lot for he and his wife. He actually gave me the correct dollar and cent amount. In that split second, my mind flashed back to my Sunday School and the purposes and ways of angels and the verse in Hebrews slammed into my brain like a train. Without a second thought, I pulled out my wallet and handed the guy what he asked for, plus a few extra dollars since I didn't have the correct change (go figure . . . . that's probably when God chuckled). And, most amazing of all, the man thanked me in God's name and I left the building whistling Christmas carols.

For at least this one time, I listened to my heart (meaning God) and not my head (meaning my pride and selfishness). And for this one time, I was blessed probably more than the man to whom I gave the money. Did he really use it for getting to his car? I don't know. Did he use it to buy a burger, beer or some type of drugs? I don't know. But, I do know that I gave him the money with God's purpose in mind, so in some way He will be glorified.

I'm a better person tonight. I still have my Ipod® close at hand and still know plenty of phrases in Spanish, French and Jimmy-ese, but I do know that I will be more receptive to the language of God in the coming days.

As it is written, "There, but for the grace of God, go I."

And for today my friends, this has been the gospel according to Jimmy.

What a Day!

It seems that in most of the major events of my life, I am not content with just the mundane and routine way of doing things. Drama and Flair always seems to accompany me. Such as was the day of my retirement. It apparently wasn't enough to retire from a good job and have a nice drive home reflecting on the friendships and good times. Oh no, THAT would be far too ordinary for me. I just had to spend my last commute sideswiping a telephone pole and rolling my SUV almost three times and slinging all the contents of my 28 years all over the road and sidewalk. Yeah, that's me, do it with Flair! The police came, the paramedics came, and they picked glass out of my arm, scalp and legs, flushed more from my eyes, made me perform all types of balancing acts and realized I was not seriously injured to warrant a trip to the closest ER.

All frivolity and joking aside, I cannot comprehend how I walked from this wreck without serious injuries or even death. In an attempt to avoid the car in front of me (which stopped suddenly), I steered toward the sidewalk, hit the telephone pole and began the rolling that my mom always worried about. As I saw the windshield shatter and begin caving in, I covered my face with my hands and arms, lowered my head to rest on the steering wheel and put myself in God's hands. When it all ended, I realized that though I was bloody and contorted in a position not normally found in nature, I was alive. Four good Samaritans were already at the car and helped me out through the windshield, called the police and picked up some of my belongings from the highway.

All the police and paramedics were amazed that I was alive and basically uninjured. I told them it was God protecting me. A lady walking down the sidewalk looked around the car and asked if the driver was alive. I told her it was me and I seemed to be fine. She started to cry and asked if she could give me a hug and say a prayer for God's blessing and protection. So, there on the side of a major highway in Friday traffic, this big ole white guy was hugging, praying and crying with a little skinny black lady. She was the angel I needed at that moment. She was from the projects nearby; I live in the suburbs. Her shoes were full of holes and ragged; mine were Doc Martens that probably cost more than she has to buy groceries for a week. Her clothes were ill-fitted and tattered; mine were Ralph Lauren and Izod. Yet, she was praising God that this man she has never met or will ever see again was safe She didn't see me as a person, just as a child of God. The hug, the tears and the prayer led me to realize that God was still in charge of my life and definitely has more for me to do.

The next day when I went to the tow yard to finish cleaning out the car, the young man who led me through all the wrecked and junk cars was also amazed that I was in decent condition. As I walked around to the driver's side to reach in, he made the comment that "obviously that cross and fish on my rear bumper protected me . . . or rather, the One who they represent kept me from being hurt." Again, an angel of sorts reminded me of God's protection from harm and that more and better things are yet to come.

Since last weekend, the soreness and stiffness lessens each day, the bruises are fading and most of the glass has finally worked itself out of my scalp and arm. My body is healing, but my soul is still feeling very unworthy of God's mercy and protection. I know I don't deserve the blessings I have and especially the blessing of walking away from this wreck, however, on several occasions these past few days, the scripture from Jeremiah 29:11 has been interjected into my life. God has plans for me (*and for you*), plans for good and not for harm. Today I have another vehicle to drive and a new beginning in my life. But most importantly, I have been reminded rather Dramatically and with Flair that *"God is Good . . . all the time. And all the time . . . God is Good!"*

And so for today with a most grateful heart, this has been the gospel according to Jimmy.

Refuge From The Storm

"The Lord is good, a stronghold in the day of trouble, and He knows those who take refuge in Him." (Nahum 1:7)

Our area has been buffeted by severe storms over the past couple weeks. Heavy rain, lightning, thunder and even hail has swept through my part of the county, sometimes with almost no warning. Blue skies overhead one minute, then CRACK! The sky is dark, the thunder rolls and the deluge begins. As long as I am inside, the storms don't usually cause me great alarm, however, I was caught on the golf course last summer when one of these storms arose. The four of us were quite concerned for a few moments. How many odds were against us, standing as we were in the middle of an open fairway, almost underneath a set of power lines with metal golf clubs in our hands? When we saw the first lightning bolt strike in a yard adjacent to our location, all we remember doing was throwing our clubs up in the air and falling to the ground screaming like a bunch of school girls. Finally, it occurred to us that perhaps we should look for shelter. Even though I was with three close friends, I really didn't relish the thought of being flash-fried with them. My idea of death was much more warm and fuzzy and involves being surrounded by nice music, family and friends.

My dog, Murphy, is much the same way. At the first sound of thunder, he immediately switches into 'storm mode.' This consists of bugging his eyes out as far as possible, flattening his ears back until they almost touch behind his head and shivering fast enough to churn butter. At this point, he tries to find a place to get away which usually involves trying to tunnel underneath me wherever I might be. Failing to do that, Murphy will settle for crawling under a pillow on the sofa, underneath the coffee table or under his favorite beach towel. So, there I sit in the midst of a storm with a shaking beach towel in the middle of my living room that begins to whine and howl as the storm gets closer and closer. He will not let me pick him up. My attempt just seems to add to his anxiety level, so I leave him alone and try to calmly talk him through the towel. If I make the attempt to pass a treat under the towel, all I get is a snarl. We had a tornado alert one night a few years ago and the attempts to get both Murphy and me into a bathtub with a mattress, flashlight and radio was just hilarious beyond description.

What is your 'storm mode' when the storms of life begin to buffet you? Are you like Murphy and try to hide and get away? Are you like me and fall face down on the ground screaming like a banshee? Or, as the scriptures suggest, do we take refuge in God, our Stronghold, our Shelter? We face so much these days with illnesses, deaths, job loss, divorces, drugs and crime that there is no place to hide and we cannot ignore these storms. Our human capabilities are not able to weather everything life throws at us, nor are we able to fully comfort those who are going through the trials. Only God can do this. Only God can provide us with shelter and comfort. Only God can speak the words which can take away the pain and fear. Only God can provide the power of Love to protect us. Many times we do not feel His presence, and that is normal and expected. However, that does not mean He is not there guiding and guarding us all the way through. Then, when we finally come through and awake into the day of sunlight once again, we can look back and see that God never left our side.

My closing thoughts? It was a very stupid thing to be on a golf course during a thunderstorm, and I wish I could say it would never happen again, except that my friends and I are rather dense. But, this I can say, God will always be my protector and stronghold in the thunderstorms of my life. He has done it **faithfully** for many years and I have the faith to know that He will continue for years to come (well, unless I insist on playing golf in the rain with friends who have no common sense).

> *"When you pass the the waters, I will be with you;*
> *and through the rivers, they will not overflow you.*
> *When you walk through the fires of life, you will not be scorched,*
> *nor will the flame burn you. For I am the Lord your God,*
> *the Holy One of Israel, your Savior." (Isaiah 43:2-3)*

And for today my friends, this has been the gospel according to Jimmy.

Being Icebound with
a Neurotic Single Guy

If you are someone like me who registers on the Obsessive Compulsive Personality side of the meter then finding yourself basically snow and ice-bound for two days is not a pretty thing. Several inches of ice had fallen which for all intents and purposes shut down most of North Georgia. So, there I sat on Saturday morning absolutely delighted to have a couple of days at home to catch up on DVD's which I had not watched, several books I had not read and spend some quality time with Murphy (who would much rather have had me gone for the day).

However, as I said earlier, somewhere between the third and fourth hours of "Harry Potter" movies, the OCP syndrome began to rear its head. I had gone into the bathroom to get some scissors from the drawer when I noticed how messy the drawer was and how the long items (like scissors) were all jumbled up with the short items (like tweezers). How can I finish a movie with a drawer in that state? So, I spent a very happy few minutes getting the drawer back into shape using appropriately sized containers. Then, as I was finishing up, I opened one of the lower cabinets beneath the sinks and what to my horror?? The shampoo and soap samples which I had collected from motels were not lined up against the cabinet wall as they should be, but some had fallen over, some were turned with the labels not showing and they were actually all mixed up together, not separated by soap, shampoo and lotion. While I was down there, I managed to throw away a lot of other accumulated junk which had gone unnoticed over the past few years and finally had the cabinets and drawers in that bathroom in such a wonderful organized manner that I could finally go back to Harry. Well, after I cleaned and washed out my hairbrush and put a new brushtip on my electric toothbrush, which has the little color coded ring that gave me some difficulty in finding one to match the hand towels.

As soon as I sat down on the sofa with Murphy curled up beside me and I pressed the Resume Play button, my eyes were instantly drawn to a couple kitchen cabinet doors which were slightly open. How can anyone watch a movie with their cabinet doors open? So, as I got up to go close them, I just HAD to restack to the dishes according to size and pattern then move on to the magazine rack so that I could put the magazines in alphabetical order first, then date order within that grouping. We won't even go into the alphabetizing the spice and herb cabinet.

As I was bundling up the trash to take out to the garage from my morning (now afternoon) playtime, I caught sight of myself in the mirror and realized how badly I needed a haircut. With an icestorm raging outside, I doubted that my local barber would be there, and (heaven forbid) I should have to wait two days until they opened, so off I trudged back to the bathroom where "I know I can cut my own hair! After all, I have sat and watched them do it for many years!". Needless to say, I now know why I pay as much as I do for a haircut and realize the value of training and internships in that field.

So, finally after I had done all the above, plus rearranged most of the living room, sun room and hall closet, and did some touchup painting from my furniture shoving, I finally finished my Harry Potter marathon and moved on to the others in my "need to be watched" box.

Such was my weekend. For the life of me, I cannot come up with any deep spiritual or theological thoughts or implications to my rather OCP and ADHD lifestyle, except to just say that God loves us all . . . . He doesn't care what our syndromes or our neuroses are . . . . He just loves us. And, I for one, am very thankful.

And for today my friends, this has been the gospel according to Jimmy.

People of Vision

Back in the spring of 1973, I was strolling along the sidewalks of Old Towne Augusta, Georgia while spending the weekend away from college with friends. Up ahead, we saw the neon flashing sign proclaiming, "Ask Madame Lucia—She Knows Your Future." What college kid can avoid such an enticing thing as having your fortune read by some (gifted) woman on a hot Saturday afternoon along the riverfront in an old eastern Georgia town? So, we went in, plunked down a few dollars before Madame Lucia (who looked old enough to be qualified as "Crone Lucia"), and watched as she began the process of looking at our palms and into her somewhat smudged crystal ball to determine the futures of three rather clueless college boys. Needless to say, I never met and married a hot girl named "something starting with an S," my bank account has never gotten into the six figures (even counting the decimal), and all my limbs are still attached. Did I think Madame Crone could really have a vision about my buddies or me? Nah, it was just something fun to do, but as we've kept in touch through the years, we often go back to the vision Lucia had for us and share a good laugh.

Is it possible for people to have visions? Certainly, it is. I think of people like George Washington, Thomas Jefferson and the founding fathers of our country. Men like Lewis & Clark, Abraham Lincoln, Martin Luther King Jr., Bill Gates and even Donald Trump. Women like Clara Barton, Susan B. Anthony, Lucille Ball and yes, Oprah. These people had visions for a better world and opportunities, and then effected the changes to allow the process to begin. They did not allow the naysayers to stop them and they ignored gender and racial lines in order to make a more better society for us all (ed: yes, I know that more better isn't the most acceptable grammar, but it just seems to fit sometimes).

In Proverbs 29:18 we are told, "*Where there is no vision, the people perish.*" In his wisdom, the Teacher knew that people had to live and dream for a better tomorrow or else we would become stagnant and finally wither down to nothing and die. This is true of people, corporations and churches. We've all seen it happen and often try to place blame everywhere except for where and on whom it may be accurate.

I have been blessed over the past seven years to be part of a church with a visionary pastor and staff. I daresay that a day, or probably an hour, has not passed that Pastor Rick is not thinking of a new ministry and a more effective way for our church to reach our community for Christ. Never compromising the Scripture and never bowing to the current trends of "entertainment worship," our pastor leads his staff and congregation with the integrity and transparency of a true man of God. Before you think that all is rosy and wonderful in the land of Salem, there are those who do not agree or do not understand the direction we may head. However, they are (usually) faithful enough to hang around, continue supporting the church and not do a lot of harm. I have learned that a true visionary always anticipates the negative aspects, keeps his or her ear tuned to the people and is willing to discuss and listen to those with concerns. A person with vision is also unafraid of positive confrontation in order to smooth the path for all peoples. As one of my heroes once said, "The needs of the many often outweigh the needs of the few."

I think that God has given us all a degree of vision. It may be for our family, our jobs, our hobbies and pastimes, our friendships or for our churches. If we are receptive to His vision for our lives, then we will have success. If we ignore or stifle the vision God has given us, then our spirit dies. I am the first to admit that I have not always been the most receptive to God's vision for my life and I've dealt with the consequences.

Whose vision should I follow—Madame Lucia or God? Not one thing that Madame Lucy told came true, plus she charged me $5. Everything God has told me has come true and His gift doesn't cost me a penny. He paid the price through His Son, Jesus. So, again, is it Lucia or God? It's up to you.

And for today my friends, this has been the gospel according to Jimmy.

The Thugs Meet the Geezers

Just when you start to think that the world is going to hell-in-a-hand-basket, a scene at a local restaurant in the McDonough Square showed several of us that we still have a toehold on all things good and true.

Several weeks ago, two friends of mine were eating at one of the local eateries on the square with several member of their family, all senior adults. They had not been together for a long time, so there was much catching up and laughing involved during their luncheon and some younger and tougher-looking construction-type workers who were also eating noticed this frivolity.

Now, in many places around the country, this could have easily led to a confrontation between the generations about whose right to a quiet lunch was being violated. At some point during the meal, the tough guys commented to the senior adults about the fun they seemed to be having and a congenial conversation followed. This in itself was a good thing, but the best was yet to come.

The young tough guys finished their meal, paid their bill and said good-bye to the older folks and wished them a good day. A short time later, to the surprise of the senior adult group, the waitress came over and told them that the younger guys had paid their food bill in full and said the guys remarked that when 'they were that age that they hoped to be able to have so much fun."

Who saw that coming? We see all the growth in Henry County and all the diversity that growth brings to our communities. Unless we can learn to understand and accept these differences in religion, ethnicity, lifestyle, economics, etc, then we will become like so many of our counties to the north. Again, who wants that to happen?

The young tough-looking guys at lunch could have easily been misconstrued as thugs, gang members, or redneck trash. But, they were not. They were nice young men who work hard for a living with families and friends just like you and me. The senior adults in the same restaurant could have been seen as a bunch of loud old geezers who ought to stay at home and not be on the roads. Not so, because they are family who enjoyed getting together and catching up on a sunny day in McDonough. When the groups met, a simple word called respect came into existence.

Aretha (and the Beatles) introduced us to the term several decades ago, but God gave it to us several centuries ago. The basic word here is "RESPECT (a/k/a) LOVE." Love others, treat them as you want to be treated, and don't judge others because you may be judged yourself. These are all words that God gave us by which to live. So your neighbors look or live differently than you. Respect them and try to find some common ground on which to meet. Someone has a crying child in a restaurant or store? Don't give them evil death looks, but put yourself in that parent's shoes for a second and smile. Let them know you do have some compassion in your heart for their struggle.

Do you promise to try harder this week? Promise? I hope you will because I can promise that you'll make a world of difference in someone's life. Just like the group who had their meal paid for few weeks ago. They are still talking about those nice young men and how it made their day.

And for today my friends, this is the gospel according to Jimmy.

From the Mouth of a Child

One of the advantages of living in a fairly small town is that you can go spend the evening at the ballpark and know most of the people there. They either go to your church, or live in your neighborhood, shop in the same grocery store or you see them at some of the local restaurants. It is a good way to spend a spring evening when you just want to be outside to just go sit and watch some softball games.

Last week, I was at the ball field to watch several of our church teams play. As the schedule worked out, two of our teams will play each other in the upcoming weeks. When this was discovered, it became a point of discussion between everyone and the good-natured taunting began. During the midst of all the talk and threats, Joe's oldest son, Hunter, came up to him and asked, "Dad, do you mean that two teams from Salem will be playing each other?" Joe replied that this was correct to which Hunter replied, "So, then it doesn't really matter who wins, does it?"

That one simple remark from a young boy caused me to think about how much more wisdom he had that many of the adults in the crowd (I almost said congregation. That's curious). There will be those who take that game seriously and want to win so that it is known that they beat the other church team and beat them badly. There will be those who continue to rub the victory in to an extreme and cause some strain within friendships and the fellowship of a church league. There will be those who take the game far too seriously and question the umpire and coach rulings much more than they would if it were not a team from there own church on the field. However, to be fair, the large majority of folks, players and fans will see it just as a game and thoroughly enjoy the time of healthy competition. These are two teams from within our own congregation of believers, our own fellowship, so why does it have to matter so much who wins?

To go to the next step, all the teams we play are other churches in the county. Spiritually speaking, we are all part of the same fellowship of believers, just meeting in different locations. Why should that be any different than when we play against our own church teams? We are all here to primarily give praise to God, worship Him and lead others to a knowledge and awareness of Christ. We should intentionally be using our ministries as an outreach tool to reach others in our community. Yet, so often, they see two Christian church teams arguing and complaining about parts of the game to the point where their witness and testimony is harmed. We are to be "the Light, a beacon set on the Hill, set apart"; you know the scriptures. Even at church league games, there are people without Christ who need to see that there is a difference in our lives.

Hang with me folks, but, going one more step up . . . does the Christian Church get so caught up in denominationalism at times that we forget that we are all still on the same team? At times, you'll see Methodists and Baptists, Presbyterians and Assembly of Gods, all trying to compete with each other when; again, we're playing for the same team. Our paths may differ somewhat because one church sings a certain Doxology, another recites a certain Creed or Statement of Faith, one may exhibit more spiritual gifts, one may serve communion more often, but we are all still serving the same God. We're all playing on the same field, so what does it ultimately matter? Should there even be a winner when the Judgment Day comes? Will God reward the Baptists because there are more of them there than there are from another Christian denomination? I don't think so. My Bible says that we will ALL stand before the Throne, not sorted into denominational entities. No one's house will be bigger than another just because you might use real wine instead of grape juice (or in the case of one of my churches whose pastor called for a communion service at the last minute . . . . we got Crystal Light Tea in the little plastic cups).

We need to just chill out and enjoy the games of life. Enjoy the fellowship with fellow believers in other congregations. Enjoy the walk with God, laugh with Him as He teaches us what he need to learn (for I know He laughs at some of my mishaps), let Him take us where He wants, smell the smells and hear the sounds that He brings our way, just relax in His arms and go with the ride. It will be more exciting than anything you can find at any amusement park. This, my friends, I can promise.

When we can come to that day, then I do not believe it will really matter who wins.

And this, my friends, is the gospel according to Jimmy (and Hunter).

Diversity in Aqua-World

In most pet stores, fish are groups in tanks labeled 'community fish,' 'semi-aggressive fish,' and 'mean as pit bull fish.' Ideally, you should not mix the occupants in your home aquarium without creating a war to rival anything the Middle East is now seeing. Being a person who enjoys diversity in groups of people, I figured that would translate to the fish world, also. Here's what my experiment in fish tank diversity taught me after a day of fish shopping.

One, just because a 'semi-aggressive' shark looks nice and gentle does not mean that after a few weeks he won't begin hiding underneath the rocks and plants in wait for innocent tetras and guppies. Swoosh! One quick dart and Mr. Tetra is missing part of a tail. Another dart later in the day and Mrs. Platy just lost a fin and part of her side. At this point, none were life-threatening attacks, but it was rather sad to see this happen, so Mr. Shark went to his own bowl to live alone until he can get along with others.

Then, I noticed that behind the miniature Parthenon in the back of the tank, apparently I had a "Brokeback Aquarium" movie being filmed. These two same-gender guppies were seemingly canoodling a little too much for the appropriateness of my water world environment. I have tried all manner of ways to keep them separated and to interest them in other inhabitants, but they always seem to wind back behind the Parthenon. What's a guy to do?

The first of the week, Mrs. Platy began to pop out the babies one evening and I noticed with horror that some of the other fish seemed to consider these tiny creatures as food and were poised behind Mama Platy gobbling up her younguns as fast as they could. I rushed to her rescue and after moving her to a separate container, managed to keep the rest of her brood intact.

I have a number of different species of fish in the aquarium. Most of them just get along with each other regardless of breed, color or gender. A few cause problems, but they are in the small minority.

How diverse is your neighborhood, your workplace, your city, your shopping and restaurant favorites? Growing up as a teenager in the 1960s, I can remember the efforts to create diversity in school and neighborhoods and the violence that sometimes erupted. However, I can also remember when my high school first experienced a diverse student body that we really didn't seem to notice anything different. These students were our neighbors, played in the band with us, sat with us at lunch, etc. We didn't make an effort to be accepting . . . . it just happened.

Our neighborhoods, schools and churches still seem to have a problem with areas of diversity, but it is not always an ethnic problem. Do you have people of different religions as neighbors who may wear different style clothing that makes them "different?" Are there any folks that you pass in the stores or restaurants that obviously may not be as well off financially as you? These are all situations of diversity.

Do we act like the shark in my tank and dart in and out nibbling at them by gossip, innuendos and ignorance until they are living a crippled existence? Do we punish their children for what we perceive as the problems with the parent or parents? Do we refuse to wave or acknowledge them thinking that if we ignore them, then they really cease to exist?

What did Christ teach? Love your neighbor as yourself. In Him there is no Jew or Greek (or Gentile). In the big sheet vision to Peter, we are taught that all creatures, including humans, are acceptable to God and we should follow that example. Now, I'm not suggesting that we go up to all our diverse neighbors and passer-bys, grab them with a big hug, kiss 'em and tell them that we love them. Just do as Christ did. He went about doing good, loving all people regardless of social standing, ethnicity and lifestyle (remember the naked demon possessed man, the woman accused of adultery, the prostitutes, etc).

None of us are better or worse in God's eyes than those around us. He equally loves us and He expects, no, He commands us to love each other as He loved us. If you can rationalize around that one, then good luck.

My aquarium is a diverse place; a community of harmony as a general rule, but occasionally some fish disturbs the peace. In my god-like role to them, I can just flush the troublemakers. What more can God do to us?

Oh dear, as I sit here tapping away, the guppies are heading back to the Parthenon.

And for today my friends, this has been the gospel according to Jimmy.

"Hey, Mr. Jimmy. This is Tonya."

This was my introduction to a lady almost a year ago that would prove to teach me much about determination, strength and character.

"I just got laid off my job and need just a few dollars to pay my phone bill this month. I really hate to ask, but I really need just this little bit until I can get work."

Everyday in my job I deal with people who need assistance for various and sundry things. Rent, utilities, clothes, gasoline, food, somewhere to live, a job, medical care and almost everything that we take for granted in our daily lives. We try to help out as best we can, as do other churches and agencies, but funds are short and the needs are great.

As I talked and helped with Tonya more and more over the past year, her story unfolded to me and I realized this lady had more life than most folks I know. She has no transportation, so she rides a bike everywhere she goes; and I mean everywhere. From the McDonough Square up Hwy 155 to the East Lake area to try and find work and then back again. She had a serious drug and alcohol problem until four years ago when she got herself clean, but her face shows the harsh scars of knife fights and beatings during that period of her life. Her priority is to remain clean, and find a long-term job so she can take care of herself without asking for more help.

As the year passed, Tonya and I spoke of her broken family, of her problems in the past and her efforts to get a break in life. I rarely spoke to her about the need of God's place in her heart because she needed some physical food and shelter before she could begin to understand about God's love and provision. She could not relate to a loving Heavenly Father when all she had known in her earthly life had been verbal and physical abuse, crime and isolation. Perhaps I was wrong, but I felt she needed more at the moment than spiritual talk when her stomach was growling and she still had a seven-mile trip on a bicycle to get home. But, each time we talked, we would have a prayer.

Last week, Tonya showed up at my office beaming as she excitedly told me that she was leaving her man and moving to a shelter where they would help her stay clean, find her a job and set her up in an apartment when she was ready to be on her own. All she had on her bike was a paper bag with some clothes and a couple pictures. She spoke sadly of leaving her house and belongings, but was thrilled at the anticipation of a brand new start in her life. Her smile and the glistening tears on her cheeks made the knife scars invisible and I saw a true child of God standing there waiting for a new life. She said that she knew God was working in her life and she was ready to finally listen. We were crying as we walked her out the door to her bicycle where she put a new Bible we gave her into her basket and rode off to start a new life.

She promised to keep in touch, but we all know how that goes. What I do know is that a lady named Tonya entered my life last year needing assistance and she gave far more to me than I ever provided for her.

"Then Jesus said, if you have provided for any of My Children, then you have provided for Me." (Matthew 25:40)

And for today my friends, this has been the gospel according to Jimmy.

Just Me and God

Thinking Back, Looking Forward

My parents recently bought some new furniture for their screen porch and I inherited a pair of old metal chairs in the process. These chairs are as old as I can remember and are the good substantial type of chairs that you can no longer buy. I remember many evenings and weekends spent on the back patio or the front porch sitting in these chairs just watching cars go buy, watching planes fly over and waving to all the neighbors when they passed. In those chairs, I dreamed of 'what I was going to do when I grew up,' studied for school, visited with family and friends, watched my sister flirt with the guy working on the street sewers and, well, you can tell the chairs saw a lot of our family life.

Today has been a great day in the Atlanta weather scene, the type of day we long for when the hot and muggy summer finally arrives in full force. I was sitting out on my front walk this evening and as I slightly rocked back and forth, my mind drifted back to so many things from days gone by that I miss and will never experience again. It was not a maudlin time of sentimentality, but an enjoyable walk down memory lane. So, without further ado, here's my top list of things I miss the most:

1. Starting with the obvious, I miss the full, thick head of hair I had in earlier years.
2. I miss playing outside until after dark with the neighborhood kids and hearing all the screen doors slam open; as our moms would call us home in unison.
3. I miss playing the outdoor games like "Swing Statue," "Red Light," "Red Rover," Wiffle Ball and the skateboard of my generation that was a 2x4 with your old metal roller skates (you know, the kind with the skate key) nailed to the bottom of the board. You couldn't turn or maneuver; you just went where gravity took you.
4. I miss the thrill of going to Sunday school in the children's department because you knew there would be a cool flannel graph lesson and Kool-Aid and butter cookies to stick on your fingers.
5. I miss eating dinner with my family every night around our old rectangular pine table my dad built. No television was allowed during meals (and still isn't) and now I realize now that the 'forced' communication between us was more important than staring at a (then) small black & white screen.
6. I miss our Saturday night rituals of Spaghetti for supper, watching "Lost in Space" afterward, baths for all, then studying our Bibles and putting some change in our offering envelopes for church the next morning.

7.   I miss the innocence of childhood, when I believed that Live Atlanta Wrestling was real and when there was an actual Birthday Bunny to bring presents (what can I say . . . my family is a bit on the freelance side).

8.   I miss catching lightning bugs in a jar, chasing small frogs down the street, swinging on a rope swing across the creek, sitting in our tree house with my girlfriend and reading Hardy Boy (me) and Nancy Drew (her) books, riding go-carts all over the neighborhood, and taking swimming lessons in a pretty nasty green-tinted pool.

9.   I miss the education of all levels of school; elementary, secondary, university and seminary. My mind thrives on stimulation and I never want it to grow stale.

10.   I miss the thrill of learning to play the piano, the awesome revelation that this gift came from God and the worship that it still brings me each Sunday as I play for my church.

11.   I miss the days when all we had to worry about was whether to buy Goobers or Raisinets at the movie house down the street, not whether the language was going to be foul or the violence too gruesome. Kids today grow up far too quickly.

12.   I miss PONG, my first Apple IIE computer and my favorite fountain pen that would release my mind and heart onto paper.

13.   I miss cruising up I-16 and I-75 on the way home from college, windows down on my '65 Chevy Impala and the 8-track blasting the best tunes possible.

14.   I miss how excited I was to get my first job out of college making a whopping $100/week. I could actually go buy my own ice cream at Dairy Queen.

15.   I miss all my friends from the church youth group in high school and my gang from college. Many of them I still keep in touch with, many have passed from this life and many I always wonder where they ended up.

16.   I miss being stupid enough to think a group of juniors in high school could actually hijack a school bus for a joyride and not get into trouble.

Folks, as memory after memory flashed back while I sat rocking slowly in the front yard, I realized that no matter how cruddy things may get each day, that the SAME God who was with me during my younger years is the SAME God who is with me today. At the time many of the above was happening, they didn't seem to be so great, but now looking back they were way cool. In another few decades as I look back on these years, I know I'll be led and comforted by the SAME God as today. The SAME God who led Abraham, Isaac, Joseph and Moses . . . . who spoke to Paul on his way to Damascus . . . . who revealed himself as a man in the person of Jesus . . . who died for me (ME!), defeated the bonds of death and is now preparing a future that my human mind cannot conceive.

Think back, look forward and remember that God is the one constant through it all. Regardless of whether your life has been good, bad or tragic; if you know God personally then your hope is bright and your future is eternal.

And for today my friends, this is the gospel according to Jimmy.

Beware the Barberry

One of my favorite shrubs is the Barberry. I have several planted around my house, but the largest and nicest is at the entrance to my front sidewalk. The deep red leaves and long cascading limbs make an attractive plant, plus it is a low maintenance shrub (which appeals to me). During the winter, the foliage drops and reveals long stems covered with long thorns, so it is definitely a shrub to be respected.

Last week, I was doing a lot of work in the front shrub beds; trimming bushes, dividing hosta plants, raking out and replacing pine straw, weeding out those winter-hardy weeds, moving some rose bushes and never thinking about where the dreaded Barberry was located. All of a sudden, I felt quite a number of thorns penetrate the jeans and t-shirt I was wearing and impale me on this "favorite" shrub. After I extricated myself, I took the hedge trimmers to the Barberry with a vengeance previously unknown to myself. Afterwards, I realized that in my folly, I had only created more trimmings to pick up with thorns that penetrate even the thickest of gloves.

As I tried to get these evil thorny trimmings into the yard bag and suffering more and more thorn pricks, it suddenly dawned on me how much these stalks with thorns looked like the pictures of the Crown of Thorns that was forced upon the head of Jesus. I took a couple pieces and fashioned a circle of sorts and placed it on my head. Even when barely touching my hair, the thorns were already digging into my scalp, some of them drawing pinpricks of blood. And we know that the crown used on Jesus had thorns more like nails than like a yard shrub.

Yet, my Savior endured this Crown of Torment forced down upon His head by those with no compassion or thought for His pain. I realized that this crown was only one small part of the pain, humiliation and torture that He went through. Even after many years of belief and service to my Lord, I still cannot fully comprehend the reason. I still cannot comprehend the true meaning of the word, WORTHY. The dictionary only gives the earthly humanistic meaning and I can define it in terms of "I am worthy of getting this new job because I am the best candidate" or "You are worthy to receive this recognition because of the service you give to the community." Yet, this doesn't begin to explain to me how Jesus was worthy to die for me. This would come from a heavenly dictionary that none of us yet have access.

I sin every day. Even though this might shock some of you, it is true. I am a daily sinner. I do not deserve the friends I have, the possessions I have accumulated, the family of which I am a part, the gifts and talents which God has given me or anything other thing which is mine. I'm grateful each day for the blessings which God has given me, but I feel the sense of unworthiness. I do not deserve to be the recipient of all God has given; I do deserve the punishment for the sins I commit each day.

However, the Love and Grace of God took this punishment away from me and put it on His Son. Jesus didn't deserve it, yet He took it and bore it for me. The scriptures say the He was Worthy. Worthy to accept my sins on His head and body. That is grace, my friends. I've heard Grace defined as **G**od's **R**ighteousness **A**t **C**hrist's **E**xpense. To me, that is just a bit too cutesy for what grace really is and the true definition is still far beyond my comprehension.

> *"But God showed His great love for us by sending Christ to die for us while we were still sinners." (Romans 5:8 NLT)*

It's odd (in a funny way) how God reveals Himself in nature and teaches us lessons about Him, if we are only paying attention. I guess that having the lower half of your body invaded by Barberry thorns is the only way God could get my attention that day. Even though the concept of the Worthiness of Christ is still not fully understandable to me, I accept this gift from God and will do my best to share His message with those around me.

What does it take for God to get your attention?

And for today my friends, this has been the gospel according to Jimmy,

Don't Worry! Be God's!

"Casting all your care upon Him; for He careth for you." (I Peter 5:7 KJV)

A good friend of mine gave me a little desktop "Promises of God" so that each day I can flip a card and read a different promise that God has made to us, His children. Rather than keep it at home where things are pretty calm and serene, I decided to bring it to work where the little demons of frustration, anxiety, anger, political correctness and secularism run rampant. My thinking was that I probably needed to be reminded of God's promises more at work than at home. So far, 'tis true.

Today's promise is the verse above. As I have sat at my desk all day and see it staring at me, it is hard to not think upon the meaning. The reality of this promise has become clearer and more powerful as the day has gone on. What are your cares and worries? Job security? Not having nearly enough money for the bills? Your family? Recovering from a divorce, especially one that was very bitter? Having too little time in your day with too much to do? Feeling like you are drifting away from God? An illness of a friend, family or yourself? I'm too skinny, I'm too overweight, my hair is thinning, my hair is just not working, I'm getting older, I wish I were older, should I change jobs or stay where I am, why do some people not like me? And on, and on, and on it goes.

We have all these things that fly through our minds during the day and even keep us awake at night. We obssess and begin to lose the perspective that we need. The perspective is that we are God's children, created in His Image and He loved us enough to send His Son to die for us. Is there a greater love? Nope, not according to the scriptures. God wants us to live an abundant life, but how can we do that when all we do is worry and fret over earthly things. He wants us to love Him, love our neighbors and love ourselves, but how can we do that when our day is taken up with other emotions than the love of God? He wants us to spread His word to our friends, co-workers and those we come in contact with, but how can we do that when we aren't feeling His presence in our own lives?

Jesus promised that we could "cast all of our cares [worries, concerns, gripes, frustrations, complaints, etc] on Him, because HE CARES FOR US." He is God in Christ. He is the Creator of the universe. He is Jehovah, the God of Abraham, Isaac, Jacob and David. He is the biggest, strongest, mightiest, most powerful Being you could ever dream of existing. He can take care of you and your concerns and let you get about your job of spreading His Love to others. Think of the impact on your testimony as you tell how God freed you from the worries of this world.

Does that mean you'll never worry about anything again? Well, if you take this verse and also the promise in Philippians 4:6— *"Don't worry about anything, instead, pray about everything" (NLT)* as the truth, then the answer is no. You will never have need to worry. But, I tend to forget these promises and take the world on my own shoulders and try to fix all the problems singlehandedly. Then, finally, God will bring me to my knees and I'll turn things back to Him as I should have in the beginning. That's just the human beings that we are. But, just because we forget, God never does forget His promises to us. Read them, claim them, then Live them!

To close with a line from Annie Herring's song, "Mansion Builder,"

> *"Why should I worry, why should I fret?*
> *'Cause I've got a Mansion Builder who ain't through with me yet!"*

And for today my friends, this has been the gospel according to Jimmy.

Late Night Musings

My therapist told me one time that I had a strong tendency to make sure others were happy and content before I gave myself permission to be the same. In other words, I would settle for less for myself rather than have someone else be upset or discontent in a situation. During the process of discovering and discussing all this, it was termed the "Messiah" syndrome by my doctor, or as my mother calls it, I am the "public defender for the world."

This tendency came back to mind today because of one of the most vivid dreams I have had in years. The details of the dream aren't important, but the underlying reasons for the dream became clearer to me over the past day. In the dream, I settled for things and situations I did not really want because I didn't want others to be put out of their way.

As I reflected today on the previous chapter which discussed "worthiness," I wonder why it is that for most of my life I didn't consider myself worthy enough to be content if there are those around me who have need. I will give and give to try and help others, even to the detriment of my own needs at times. One thing I do realize is that I deal with a lot of unreal unmet expectations of myself and at times that leads to the same unreal expectations I have of those around me. At least by recognizing this, hopefully, I am getting better about it. Well, to be honest, I'm not getting better. I still expect more out of other people than they can possibly live up to because I cannot even meet my own standards most of the time. And, then I am bothered because I am expected to be the "all things to all people" person which I have always attempted to be.

Thanks be to God because He has no expectations of me other than to love Him, live for Him and tell others about Him. It is so comforting when I come into His presence because I know that I can let go of (yet) another mask and be the one with a need for once. A need for comfort, a need for compassion, a need for advice, a need to speak with honesty, and a need for total acceptance as I really am. He has *never* let me down or asked more of me than I could give.

I do not have unreal unmet expectations of God and He does not have them of me. So, why do I have them of myself and of others around me? Don't know, but the adventure continues . . . .

And for today, my friends, this has been the gospel according to Jimmy.

Perspective and Blessings

My heart is full, my mind is tired, and my body is fatigued. It has been a very full and busy day starting with a rather horrid commute to work, another mind-numbing training class on new software, a call from the vet to say that we need to increase the chemotherapy dosage for Murphy (my dog has a Pituitary gland tumor) for another 10 days, a meeting to try and mend a strained friendship and working relationship (which went well), and then to my second job at church for three music rehearsals. I left home at 7:00 a.m. and didn't get home until 10:00 p.m.

As I unwind from the day with a dog on my lap licking my elbow, my mind reflects back on all the blessings I have and a sense of contentment and thankfulness comes over me.

I am thankful for the best family in the world. We all have our quirks and oddities, but we are close and have come through some major crises together with the help of God.

I am thankful for the best church in the world. A place where God's Word is preached without apology or hesitation, a place where diversity in ethnic background, financial background and educational achievement are all welcomed and accepted, a church where the people genuinely care for each other and those around the community and world.

I am blessed by many of the teenage guys and girls who accept this old man as one of their own. I get jumped on, beat on and wrestled to the ground, but I am also hugged on, licked on (love licks), feel loved and am trusted to be honest with them and show them how much God and I love them. Thanks, kids, for all you mean to me, and most importantly, thank you parents for trusting me with your kids.

I love my Sunday school class . . . . for their diversity, for their differing opinions, for their outspoken honesty, for their love for the Lord and desire to study the scriptures and apply them to their lives.

I am humbled by the number of friends I have. In all sincerity and honesty, I am not worthy nor deserving of them. But, still they stick around and my life is so much better for them. I wish I could name them all here publicly, but they would torture me for who I would name first and the order that followed. Oh, I definitely know the order I would use, but that will never be known. So, just thanks for being my friends and for being my brothers and sisters in Christ.

However, I am aware of the perspective in all my blessings and am sobered by many things that are far beyond my little world of home, work, church and friends.

My heart still hurts for the tragedy which occured in south Asia with the tsunami. For the devastation of homes and loss of lives, I have no words with which to even pray. God, just be with those people and heal their land and homes.

It bothers me that I have young friends who have to deal with cancer and other serious life-endangering diseases. I complain because of an ingrown toenail, or because a sore shoulder has sidelined me from playing golf or tennis. Yet, these people are struggling with their daily existence and keeping a strong faith in God. That is a witness and lesson for me.

My anger arises because I know that within probably five miles of my house, there are children going to bed hungry. There are women and children being physically and verbally abused, but are not to a point where they seek help. Yet, I am sitting in a nice comfortable house with a fire in the fireplace and a sleeping dog besides me. My worry is whether to eat a bowl of ice cream or not before I go to bed.

And, I guess somewhat selfishly, it makes me sad to know my good little dog has cancer and is having to be treated with a chemotherapy pill. So far, the side effects have not been severe, but he has been my confidante and biggest fan for almost fourteen years now. He is my child, my friend, and I want his senior years to be full of quality and love.

Well, folks, perhaps I shouldn't try to write and share when I am so tired, but all these thoughts had been running around in my head and it has helped me to get them out. I would encourage anyone reading this to be aware of their blessings, for those things given to them by God for which they should be thankful. But, keep in mind the perspectives, too. The people and things that need our prayers and support, even if it means actually getting involved with their lives . . . . hmmm, novel concept isn't it? Getting involved with people in need, I mean.

As for me, I'm heading to bed. I think for the first time in several nights, I shall sleep soundly.

And for today my friends, this has been the gospel according to Jimmy.

Shhhh! God Is Trying To Talk!

"Be still, and know that I am God."(Psalm 46:10)

My physician has a phrase which he uses just about everytime he sees me. "Now Jimmy, we must learn more about age appropriate behavior." Usually this comes after a sprained wrist from volleyball, a pulled muscle from softball, a sprained ankle from a ropes course, another sprained ankle and no skin on my lower half because of learning to rollerblade. I always hang my head, act contrite and reply, "Yes, doctor. I'll try to keep that in mind."

Bwaa-haaaaa. I am one of those people who do not want to come to my last breath and have regrets for never trying things at least once. Hence, the rollerblades when I was in my late 40's . . . . an accident just waiting to happen. Finally, I came up with what I thought would be my ideal activity . . . . scuba diving. I love the water, and fish, and being wet, so I figured that I'd give it a try and take lessons. About a year ago, a local scuba company offered a beginning class, so I signed up.

Thank goodness I didn't have to wear one of those nasty wetsuits in the classes. Those would definitely not be age-appropriate behavior for me. Just a swimsuit was all that required; they furnished the rest. So, with much anticipation I went to my first class on bright summer Saturday.

Let me back up to state that I like to be involved and active in things, even though I can hold my ground as a couch potato with the best. So, my world is always in a somewhat confused state of being the spud or the stud. As a result of that, I have a very difficult time in finding a quiet time or place for God. Now, back to the scuba . . . .

The teachers introduced us to the equipment, showed us how to put it on, adjust everything and we prepared to enter the very large pond. As I submerged myself and began to breathe through the tank, I realized the power that just a flip of your foot fin had in thrusting you through the water. After a few times of practicing techniques, the teacher told us to submerge and just enjoy being underwater for thirty to forty minutes, just doing our thing. They had various items under the water for us to explore, things written out for us to read and several other activities.

The first thing I noticed was the quietness. It was absolutely still. As my breathing became regulated, I didn't even hear or notice the tank assisting my breath. All I heard was the quiet. As I paddled around the bottom of the pond like a catfish or some other bottom feeding creature, I found myself thinking about God's creation of the earth, the underwater world and the beauty therein. I discovered how to just sit on the bottom and be perfectly still. For those minutes, the truth of the above verse came crystal clear. In order to truly hear and feel God, we must be still and quiet. There on the bottom of the pond, I could feel God speaking in the quietness. Once we came back to the surface, the noises of the world seemed so very loud that I wanted to return to the pond world of quietness.

I've learned to remember that feeling as I try to commune with God these days. The feeling of being at the bottom of a body of water, feeling the presence of the water on my body, but also the overwhelming quietness of the moment. In this loud and noisy world, it is hard to "be still," but that is what God expects of us. How did he finally speak to Elijah? Not in storms and earthquakes and crashing trees, but in the gentle whisper of the wind. We have to come to that place where we can totally submerge ourselves into our God, feel His presence surrounding our bodies and to enter the overwhelming quietness of Him. Easy to do? Not at all, but once you begin to make a serious attempt, you'll be surprised at what you may encounter. Or, you can always take a scuba lesson.

And for today my friends, this is the gospel according to Jimmy.

The Curse of the Cowlick

I've never been one to care about hair. At the risk of being punched by some woman at the mall, it doesn't matter to me how much trouble a woman has with her hairstyle, as long as it looks good when she's in public. I have never read or done much research into the problems and methods of women and their hair, but one thing that I do know is that the same concern of hair appearance and style have now struck the world of men. I have buddies who own more products for their hair than they have athletic shoes. What the heck?

At first glance, you would quickly realize that my hair is certainly not my priority in life's great scheme. It stays generally short and where I can just run a brush or my fingers through it in the morning and go. The lower the maintenance, the better. Rarely does a product other than shampoo become involved in my morning ablutions and if it is a genuine bad hair day, then, well . . . that's why they make ball caps, right?

As a young boy, a cowlick plagued me. You know, that little tuft of hair that sticks straight up or grows sideways to every other hair and there is no product short of duct tape that will keep it in place. It was the bane of my existence and every adult woman that passed me would always ooh and ahh and talk about that "cute little cowlick." I hated it with a passion and was so thankful in my later teenage years when it finally went away.

Or, so I thought . . . .

I have noticed over the past couple weeks that something strange is happening in my hair. Assuming that it was just a result of my last haircut (given by myself late one night), I just glopped a little gel on it and went on. Well, the past couple of days, even the gel just laughed when it saw that spot where it was about to go. So, today I headed to the local style shop to have a professional cut this abnormality and restore my normal appearance. What to my horrified ears did she say? "Oh, I see you have a cute little cowlick up here!" NO! NO! NO! It was back. From the lurking pre-adolescent traumas of inferiority and rejection, the cowlick was back. "But, I'm in my fifties," I protested to the stylist. She laughed (laughed, mind you), "Well, sir, many times those cowlicks reappear from time to time in a person's life and it sure looks like yours is back—and with a real attitude." When I got home and began looking in the mirror, I fully expected to see the return of acne and those awful black and silver glasses that we band nerds seemed to embrace.

During the years, I have known many friends from earlier years that have left the church and are not actively serving God in any visible form. They claim to still be believers, and I cannot judge that, but their words and lifestyles do not reflect that belief. As a child, they loved and believed in God; but as they began to grow and see the world, their faith and actions came under other controls. It wasn't cool to be a believer and they began to dampen and try to contain their beliefs.

"Train up a child in the way they should go, and when they are old they will not depart from it." (Proverbs 22:6)

In this proverb, the Teacher tells us that the way we are raised as a youngster, even though we may depart from it (go into a sense of dormancy, try to quench it), when we become older we will return to the ways and beliefs of our youth. In other words, at some point, the things we wanted most to ignore once again becomes a part of our lives. God is always there and waiting for us to return to the prominent place in our lives.

As today progressed, I have tried to accept and bond with my returning cowlick. It was a part of my youth and now it has returned. Has someone you love and care for left the ways of God through the years? Claim the promise in Proverbs. Over the recent ten or fifteen years, I have seen long-time friends returning to church so that their children can learn the ways of God. They are once again worshipping and taking an active role in the life of the local fellowship. Why don't you be the cowlick in someone's life and help them return to their childhood?

And for today my friends, this has been the gospel according to Jimmy.

When the War Hits Home

"Be Strong in the Lord and in His mighty power. Put on the full armor of God so that you can take your stand against the devil's schemes. For our struggle is not against flesh and blood, but against the rulers, against the authorities, against the powers of this dark world and against the spiritual forces of evil in the heavenly realms. Therefore, put on the full armor of God, so that when the day of evil comes, you may be able to stand your ground, and after you have done everything, to STAND." (Ephesians 6:10-13 NIV)

I don't recall every hearing of spiritual warfare as a young Christian. It must have just been one of those topics that preachers avoided so as to not be thought of as heretical or something similar. Until I read recent books about the powers of darkness and the invisible battles that they wage in the world around us, I had never realized how powerful and real the angels of Satan must be. Yes, I do know these were fictional books; however, I realize how much they are based on scripture and theology.

I have had some experiences over the past year or two, and one as recent as early this morning that makes me believe that there are forces of evil trying to reach me. I don't want to go into details right now because that just keeps reinforcing the thoughts and occurences in my head and that isn't productive, especially at night.

One good thing about this is that I don't think that Satan and his forces would be particularly interested in me unless I were doing something constructive for God. My walk with Him is close and secure and I believe and am convinced that NOTHING can separate me. However, over the past few weeks and months, I have begun to seek God's will for my life much more diligently than I have before. I have written a couple times lately that I sense the leading of God in a new direction for my life happening and try to keep my wishes and goals out of the picture and leave it totally up to His leading. In addition, I also pray for the faith to accept the possibilities of starting over in new places and doing new things. God is continuing to break me so that He can fill me. If you are a Christian and have been through periods of breaking, you know this can be a tough and difficult thing because we as humans tend to resist it. When we finally give in and let God have us in total, it is a wonderful thing.

To those of you reading this, never assume that Satan and his demons are some type of fairy tale made up by scriptural authors, Dante, Sunday school teachers and preachers. Be on guard constantly if you are trying to do what God wants you to do because that is when the attacks will begin. They start out very subtle, then progress stronger and stronger until you finally give in and become a defeated Christian, bearing little if no fruit. Or, they progress until you realize what is happening and stand firm with the armor of God in place and proclaim that Jesus is Lord and through everything *"we are more than Conquerors." (Romans 8:37 NIV).*

At the risk of playing the age card, if there is one thing I have learned in my life, it is that you cannot win the war with Satan, it can ONLY be done with the armor of God in place and your trust placed in His power and strength. I have fought skirmishes in earlier years, given in and paid the price of defeat. I have also fought battles, held strong to my faith and came through victoriously with excitement, growth and renewal of my love of God. I encourage all of you to place the phrases from the above scripture on little slips of paper that you will see during the day as I have done; on your mirror at home, on the dashboard in your car, on your desk at work or school, wherever you want. **"Stand Firm." "We are more than Conquerors."**

I do ask for prayers as these days unfold. Today, I am strong in the Lord; I pray that I will be strong tomorrow, the next day and forward. That is my prayer for you, my friends.

And for today my friends, this has been the gospel according to Jimmy.

Transparencies and Masquerades

I came across a new blogsite the other day which has caused me to start thinking. The first post talks about the masks that we wear that people see instead of the real us. Then the author goes on to discuss that in front of God, there are no masks, because God can see through them to whom the real me is.

I began to realize that I wear masks. I have my work mask, my church mask, my 'with these friends' mask, my 'with those friends' mask and my 'with family' mask. And at times, I realize I even have my 'just being at home with me' mask because with so many roles and so many masks to juggle it takes effort to keep them in place and it isn't easy to let them go. However, on occasion, when it is just me and God, I let all the masks drop and I remember the boy and man I am and that I really do like him a lot and wonder where he is much of the time.

Which leads me to the question; do people know who I am? Do they know the type of music I really prefer? Do they know my favorite colors? Do they know what really annoys me and what doesn't? Do they know the situations and circumstances I have been through in life (and still have to deal with), or do they not have a clue because they never asked or seemed concerned about anything other than the current moment and how it affects them? And the big question is, why do these people rarely ask me these things or want to know how and what I feel? Do they ever ask what they can do for me and how to help me through a rough time, or do they just want me to be who THEY want me to be and do not want to rock the boat because of the masks that THEY themselves are wearing. And, yes, YOU are wearing masks because I can see them at times which concerns me that perhaps you can see mine as well, but we all treat them like the proverbial pink elephant in the living room.

Perhaps the real me is just a melding of all the different masks into a totality of being and the real Jimmy is alway there, not necessarily covered by a mask, but just using different gifts, abilities and talents for the given situation. Way down inside where it is just me and God, there are no masks. I know myself fairly well, but God knows me far better. He knows you far better than you can ever know yourself, too. That is a comforting thought for me because it is nice to know that there is always a place where no masks are required; there will be no masquerade ball before Jehovah God.

I, for one, am excited because through these past few days of self-discovery, I have rediscovered the man I am and have realized that I am fairly much on track with what I think God's plan has been for me all along. It's an interesting thought and concept . . . . masks, that is. Are they necessary at times? Never? Do we really want to be transparent or to see the true people around us? I don't know. As for me, I'll be working on the masks. Changing the size, perhaps, making them smaller while adding some unique touches like feathers, beads and macaroni noodles. Who knows?

And for today my friends, this has been the gospel acording to Jimmy.

The Intruder

I always made the assumption that my car would be safe in the garage. After all, I had a garage with no windows, a door that shuts and locks, plus a motion detector light on the outside. The other night was like every other night. I pulled into the garage, shut the door behind me, left the windows slightly open since it was so hot inside the garage and went into the house for the night.

The next morning, I opened the garage door and got into the car as always. Everything seemed normal so I suspected nothing unusual as I backed out of the driveway and headed downtown to my day job. However, as I entered the heavier traffic a couple exits away, I caught a movement in the rearview mirror just behind my right shoulder. Instinctively, I glanced back and my heart froze as I saw the intruder.

If there is one thing in this world that will cause me to run screaming like a schoolgirl, it is a spider. And, that's what was dangling from the overhead light of my car on its sinister web of death. I could tell that its eyes were fixated on me as the victim du jour on today's menu. Not knowing how it happened, I managed to exit the expressway without creating havoc, opened the door and left my SUV to the spider. He could have it. After a moment or two when I began to breathe somewhat normally, I peered in through the side window and realized that the creature of horror was not the size of a basketball (which is what I first imagined), but more like a fingernail. Well, actually more like a pinky toenail. Since I live in the neighborhood and knowing that friends and neighbors could be driving by, I decided I needed to maintain some dignity and rid my car of the beast. I had an umbrella in the back, so I retrieved it quickly and started to poke the spider through a partially opened window. It glowered at me a time or two and then started to run up its own web for safety. With one more well-timed poke, I made contact and to my horror, the spider jumped onto the umbrella and began racing up through the window and toward me. Now, the screaming schoolgirl entered the picture; slinging the spider-laden umbrella down the bank, I jumped back into my car and took off feeling quite victorious and smug because I had defeated this threat to my life, limb and to the world. I'm da man!

Now, how many times do we allow the little things that creep (no pun intended) up on us in life to totally destroy our moments? Like I said, in reality this spider was quite tiny, but to me, it was huge and threatening. I allowed it to disrupt my morning and throw my stress levels into overdrive. Do you wake up with a fairly enthusiastic attitude about facing the day and then the coffeepot doesn't work and it instantly throws you into an ill mood? When your well-designed plans for the day are abruptly changed, can you handle it without getting all snarky? Do you have a struggle getting yourself or your family ready on Sunday mornings to the extent that you are so frustrated that even if God whacked you with a bat, you still wouldn't feel His presence? Do you obligate yourself to so many things that you become so stressed that you cannot enjoy any of them? Does that one annoying person always seem to find you at the restaurant and whine on and one so that you can't even digest your food? We are told in I Peter 5:7 to "give all your worries and fears to God, because He cares for us." and Philippians 4:6 says "don't worry about anything, instead, pray about everything" (NLT). God is concerned with every aspect of our lives from the major things to the tiny irritating things. I think that even includes spiders.

And for today, that is the gospel according to Jimmy.

Family, Friends and
General Dysfunction

No, I Do Not Dye My Hair!!

I have a rather odd picture on my desk. It is a picture of my mother with a goat. Does the fact that my mother had her picture taken with a goat surprise me? Not a bit. You just have to know my mother. I guess the only thing surprising is that there is only a goat and not a goat, a giraffe and a pig. Again, you just have to know my mother. Now, before you say anything I need to warn you that I am a mama's boy. And there is one thing you do not do around a mama's boy and that is . . . . to talk about his mama. My mother is probably one of my best friends. She helped raise me in the Lord and encouraged my love for music so that now I have made one album and play keyboard for one of the larger churches in metropolitan Atlanta. She has been my comfort in dark days and the first to call when things are going great. To put it simply, my mother is a woman of God. There is a verse in Proverbs which puts it plain and simple.

"Gray hair is a crown of Glory; it is gained by living a righteous life." (Proverbs 16:31 NLT)

Thinking back over my life, most of what I have learned has come from people with gray hair; those who have lived a life for more years than I and have learned how to walk closely with God. They have been my encouragers, my supporters, my prayer warriors, and, when necessary, my rear-end kickers. So many times, our society and churches tend to overlook the value of the gray-haired people and, even sadder, often they overlook their own value, too. You have heard it said, "I've been doing that for years, it's time for somebody younger to do it." "Oh, honey, I'm just too old to keep the nursery or preschoolers now." "My goodness, those children don't want an old person like me teaching them. Get somebody younger who they will like."

Hogwash!! The last I knew, God did not give out pink slips or early retirement options. Children, teenagers and adults NEED to have older people around to help guide and mentor them. Who else can help you through the difficulties of marriage when it is going sour? Who else can encourage you through the traumas of raising children either with or without a spouse? Who else understands the loss of a spouse to death? The gray-headed people can, that's who. They've lived it. They know that God can bring you through world wars, through depressions (both financial and emotional), through rocky relationships, through the days when you want to toss your children out the back window and through days when your faith is low and your world is dark. They know and they can help.

My hair is turning gray. Usually it is cut short so that the gray mixed in with the brown is more visible, but as it grows out the darker hair begins to cover the gray. There are a couple teenagers at church who will start teasing/harrassing/annoying me with hollering across the most crowded restaurants: "Look! Mr. Jimmy is dying his hair again! Where'd all that gray hair go? C'mon, Mr. Jimmy, admit it!" Of course, the more I protest and deny, the louder they get (all in fun and love I keep telling myself).

But, I do not dye my hair. I am proud to be turning into a gray-head, because it means that I have been through life experiences and God is weaving me a crown of glory. As I have written before, I am proud to be one of the adults that the teenagers come to when they have problems or concerns and need some advice. They know they can trust me to be straight with them and keep their confidences. They know I'll be honest with them, even when they don't like the honesty. And the cool thing is that they come to this gray-head on their own.

So, I do not dye my hair and never will. I am proud to be a Gray-Head for God. In fact, maybe I'll do T-shirts and ballcaps . . . . and those little tote bags you hang on your walkers and wheelchairs . . . . and a whole line of shuffleboard and bocci ball equipment . . . . and probably some rollerblades just for good measure.

And so for today my friends, this is the gospel according to Jimmy.

Go Ye Therefore—by Instant Messenger, Blogs and Text Messages

Through the fog of almost sleep, I heard the ring of a phone. I glanced over at the clock next to my bed and it read 12:17 a.m. Once again, the ringing came, but I realized that it was not coming from the phone on the end table, but from elsewhere in the house. Through my groggy state, I realized it was an instant messenger alert. Someone was calling me through the computer in my study. The sensible thing to do was to ignore it, which I tried to do, however my curiosity finally got the better of me and I knew I might as well get up and go see who it was. Plus, their constant attempt to contact me was only going to drive me to a criminal act if it continued.

I recognized the screen name immediately as one of the teenagers at church. I replied to him with a rather snarky "WHAT! It's after midnight, dude! Go to bed!" His reply almost stopped my heart. He was in a tough spot—a really bad place—and needed some help. Not financial help (as in bail bond), but spiritual. He felt as if he were losing his way and needed someone to talk to in hopes he could find himself and God again. Peer pressure was getting too strong; he was making some bad choices and knew the consequences would be coming. He did not feel like God would let him come back and he felt so terribly alone even though he was in his home with parents and siblings. You know, that kind of alone that you can feel when God seems so far away and the road ahead seems too far and so dark and so lonely. It is night and the fears increase as the shadows come and the thoughts of sleep seem impossible. You are afraid to sleep because tomorrow may actually come and that is not what you want. You cry out to God and you feel that He can't quite hear you. You are alone. Totally alone. So you reach out to someone for help. Someone, anyone, but because of your fear of rejection and judgement, you choose a seemingly anonymous route of instant messenger. Even though he knew it was me on the other end of the DSL, and I knew it was him, he was not having to admit things face to face.

We talked for a long time in that early morning conversation and when we finally signed off, he knew that God loved him as much as ever and would forgive him any transgression. He knew that God was there in his bedroom and would be watching over him as he slept. He knew that God would be there the next morning when he woke and with him all day at school. And, most importantly, he knew that God would be there when he began to change his friendships and reverse the choices he had made.

I slept very soundly that night because I knew my boy had come home to his God and would be a stronger Christian young man as a result.

I think we as Christians often miss out on many methods of ministry because we get so hung up on the traditional ways. You know, the cards, the phone calls, the visits, and so forth. There is a vast world of technology available for evangelism that is scarcely being touched. One of which are the various instant messenger services. You chat back and forth, day by day, and grow relationships with friends and neighbors that you already know. Even though it is not an anonymous service, you have that feeling and you find yourself at times being more honest and open than you would in a face to face setting. It can flow naturally into evangelistic conversations and discussions of encouragement and support.

Websites and blogs are wonderful vehicles that we use to share God with others. In just a short time, I have met brothers and sisters in Christ all across the country that I feel like I know closely even though we have never met. I am blessed by many of the writings I see, so I am certain that those who are not believers have to be impacted to a degree. As the scriptures tell us that 'some people will sow the seeds and others may help reap the harvest.' You, my fellow bloggers and scribes, are sowing a lot of seeds that God will bring to harvest.

God will bless any effort that we make on His behalf and I have been blessed by the use of technology. I certainly enjoy and prefer the personal encounters of sharing Christ with others, however, there are times that human pride may get in the way. So, we adopt strange screen names and visit websites, blogsites and instant message into the wee hours of the night. We post and comment and encourage and support people that we may never meet in person, but I kinda hope there will be a special cyber cafe in Heaven so we can connect blognames with our new heavenly faces. My friends, we should never take lightly the responsibility we have as we post and journal on our respective sites. We never know who is lurking out there and may be touched. God created the minds of people who created the advancements in technology. Let's claim it for His glory!

And that, my friends, is the gospel according to Jimmy.

The Eyes of the Man

I look into the eyes of the man and I see the boy he once was. The boy who collected insects and rocks; the boy who created art out of everyday things found in the yard and the house and the boy who always seemed intelligent far beyond his years.

I look into the eyes of the man and I see the boy who I never really knew because of the difference in our ages. The teenager who found Christ at a youth camp in Panama City, yet I did not know how to rejoice with him. The boy who seemed to look up to me for something I did not know how to give.

I look into the eyes of the man and I see the young man embarking on a career that most folks would envy. A career of prestige, social standing and importance in the community. A career that I found myself envying because the young man had the drive and ambition that I think I lacked in those days.

I look into the eyes of the man and I see the man who for a number of years grew in directions separate from his family. We never lost contact, but the contacts were sometimes few and far between. I also see the eyes of the man's mother when she would want to talk and hear his voice, yet the voice was not there.

I look into my own eyes and still see the tears shed on the night I heard of his three attempted suicides in a location far away. A location where he was alone and isolated from friends and family, yet going through a hell I will never know or can possibly imagine. I see the shock and grief in the eyes of his family and closest friends who were not aware of his plans as he made them for days ahead of time.

I look into the eyes of the man's family and friends and see the tears of relief that the attempts did not succeed and the rush of the subsequent days to gather him back home and into the arms of the familiar. Yet, I see the questions, the hurt, the terror of the "what ifs", but also the depth of love and concern for the man's welfare and recovery.

I look into the eyes of the man and see the haunted, sad look of despair and knowledge of the pain he has caused those closest to him. However, I can also see the tiniest spark of determination to rebuild his life and prove to him that he is worth living, not just for others, but also for himself.

I look into the eyes of the man and see the joy of taking one step forward, yet many times I see the pain of the two steps backward which often follow. The pain of a bi-polar diagnosis, the joy of finding a job, the hurt of not being able to handle the pressures of employment at this time, the excitement over moving home, the sadness of not knowing what his future holds.

I look into the eyes of the man and I see on a daily basis his determination to beat the demons that have plagued him and, even though slowly, very slowly, begin to defeat them and grow a little stronger in his own manhood.

I look into the eyes of the man and I see my little brother. The boy I have grown to love as we grew to be men and now, the brother I will do anything within my power to protect, defend and to help face tomorrow. I see the man who is my brother that now in many ways I look up to because I see strength within him that I'm not sure I would have had in the same battles.

I look into the eyes of my brother and see the little boy, the teenager, the young man, and now, the man of whom I am so extremely proud. I see my brother who may have wandered from the arms of God for a season, but has not forgotten the love that compels us; the love that has protected him and has brought him back to me so that I might learn from him.

Pray for my brother. He's the greatest guy in the world and I love him; and I especially want him to remember how much God loves him.

And for today my friends, this is the gospel according to Jimmy.

Dads! Gotta Love 'Em!

Hmmm, Father's Day has come again. A time to decide between a gift card to a Home Improvement store, a book, a new tie and handkerchiefs, or get really wild and find a wallet and matching key chain. I am fortunate to still have my dad living up the street from me, so I know easily that none of the above is on his 'most needed' list. Of course, he would be gracious and kind and act like it was the first gift card or book he had ever received and it was a terrific idea. That is what makes my dad, well, my dad.

My dad just turned 82 years old and is more active than most men half his age. Growing up, I remember him always being at work, being at church or being in the yard. He made sure my brother, sister and I always had a tree house, a go-cart, a rope swing or anything else that we wanted and could be built or made. He made our first skateboards out of 2x4 timber and separated roller skates. Of course, there were no turning abilities, you either went straight or you crashed. But, it would help us to "build character."

He played sports with us at home and on church teams. Even when he was old enough to retire, he was still out there catching softballs. He taught us how to ride a bicycle usually consisting of setting us on the seat, pushing us down the yard and hollering for us to "hold on and pedal. Just pedal!" Somehow, after many bandages and antiseptic ointment tubes, I managed to make it a few houses down the street without falling off.

I guess as far as physical activities go, the two that have been constant in my Dad's life is golf and bicycles. He still plays golf every week or so with some of his friends (I tend to call them the 'oldest men in the world' team) and he still rides his bicycle around the neighborhood. He decided a couple months ago that in honor of his turning 82 this summer that he would ride his bike for 82 miles. We calculated that to ride 82 miles around his cul-de-sac might tend to be a bit boring, so the family decided that the Silver Comet Trail outside of Atlanta would be a good option. Unfortunately, it was raining the week and day of his birthday and he was unable to ride. We could never tell whether he was glad or disappointed.

However, he did not give up on the idea and with the company of his sixteen-year old granddaughter he will head up to the Trail tomorrow morning. Their intent is not to necessarily ride 82 miles, but to spend the day doing two things that my dad enjoys the most—riding his bike and spending time with his family.

As this time of the year comes, I think about how important Dad has been in my life. We have locked horns quite a number of times during my life, but I knew that our disagreements did not dampen his love for me, nor mine for him. As I look back over the life of our family, his actions and motives were always to support and defend us. It was not always easy for us to understand that at the time, however looking back gives a clear picture. Thanks, Dad, for always loving me; no matter how odd you thought I might be at times. I love you.

And for today, my friends, that is the gospel according to Jimmy.

The Great Equalizer

There are few things in life that put all people on the same level of play. There are pro athletes, good athletes and pathetic athletes (my category). Upper, middle and lower economic levels; people who wear Prada and those who wear Wal-Mart; there are bosses and worker bees; and on it goes. Very few situations can bring all these diverse groups into an equality of being. One of these situations is the hospital emergency room and waiting rooms.

My dad recently had a health emergency and was rushed to the emergency room of an area hospital. Our family spent several anxious hours in the ER waiting room, the surgical waiting room and then almost a week in the ICU waiting room. Now, Dad is in a rehabilitation center and on the slow road to recovery. However, one thing I noticed over the past week is that the hospital ER and ICU puts everyone on an equal basis. This dawned on me as I was sitting next to a very professional appearing lady in designer clothes, hair styled perfectly and subtle (yet very classic) jewelry. As for myself, I had on my normal uniform of ratty cargo shorts, flip-flops, totally out of place hair and a t-shirt for some 5K-road race that I bought at the thrift store.

For those of you who have been through such, you know that after a period of time, you begin talking to people in the lobbies, waiting rooms, cafeterias and hallways of the hospital. These are people you have never seen or known before, but you have the commonality that a loved one is sick and in need of care by you and the healing professionals. You share stories and experiences, scriptures, prayers and after a few hours and days you realize how much alike we are and that we also have a concern for these other people. We have family and friends that we care about and worry when they are sick or hurt. At those times, we will reach out to others in our need for comfort and the human touch . . . . no matter how well you play sports, what label is on your clothes, how large your house and what you do for a living. My family has experienced this over the past week.

There is another Equalizer that we will all have to encounter someday. That equalizer is God. If you have read much of my work, you know that one of my big soapboxes is that of acceptance of all people regardless of any characteristics different than our own, either outward or inward. The God I know and attempt to serve is a God who sees ALL people as equal and He wants us to see them the same way. In the final days, it does not matter whether we have a huge house or a doublewide on a dirt road. Nor does it matter whether we go to church in a gorgeous state-of-the-art building or gather with believers in a home or storefront in the local strip mall. All that matters to

God, the great Equalizer, is that we love Him, love each other and treat all peoples with respect. Friends, I urge you to not spend the days we have here on earth expending the energy to judge and avoid others who appear to be different than us. When it all comes down to the basics, we're all the same.

In closing, I would like to thank all health professionals from doctors and nurses, residents and interns, lab technicians, housekeeping and volunteers. Your smiles and the pats on the shoulder make a huge difference. You are not simply in a career; you have been called to service.

And for today my friends, this has been the gospel according to Jimmy.

And It Continues . . .

It has been a rough couple of days, my friends. The toughest I've ever been through. In my last post, I mentioned that my dad had emergency surgery and was going into rehabilitation. The surgery he had was for a subdural hematoma, which meant that his skull was full of blood and fluid causing his brain to be turned and pressed against the side of his skull with such pressure he was temporarily losing some abilities like speech, vision and most movements. The surgery relieved the pressure and he began to wake up and become more aware of his surroundings after a few days. The doctors told us that in older people, as the brain shrinks the veins and capillaries become tightly stretched between the brain and skull and with some types of movements, they can begin to leak or completely break, causing the problem my dad had. Plus, the likelihood of recurrence was great.

And it did. Two days ago, my dad began to slip into a coma and was rushed from the rehab center back to the hospital ICU during the early hours of this morning. By the time my mother, brother, sister and I arrived at the hospital, the doctors had done another CT scan and once again the skull was full and the brain under much pressure and stress.

With much tears and prayers, and considering the fact he already is dealing with multiple myeloma, we chose to not put my dad through another surgery and to leave him in God's hands for what time he has left with us, which should be just a few weeks or months. He would not have the life of quality and activity which he thrived on and would be way too miserable (and cranky with us) for allowing this to happen. His quality life will now be with God and in His Heavenly home with his parents and sister who have gone before.

Tomorrow we will begin looking into a couple specific hospices which are close to home so that Mom will not be able to go back and forth without much hassle.

I wish the news were better. As the oldest son, I have had a hard day of reflection of things past and things yet to come. My nature is to be strong and not let the emotions show so that I can help the rest of the family in their need. I have always seen that as my role as the oldest child, but that role is being shaken by the events of today and of days to come.

My family will be fine. We are sorry for what has transpired and for what appears to be an inevitable outcome, but we also believe that God can perform miracles in His time and for His purposes. We have the hope that even though we do not understand that 'the peace of God will surpass all human understanding."

And for today my friends, this has been the tearful gospel according to Jimmy.

The Waiting is Hell

I sit here each night in the hospice and watch my father breath. In, out, in, out, in, out. I watch as his feet react to some reflex deep in his subconscious being and twitch a couple of times. I watch as he occasionally opens his eyes and focuses on me if I am in his line of vision. Since he is unable to move his head or body, his eyes will cut back and forth until he locates something to fixate upon. I watch, as sometimes he will move his mouth as if he wanted to tell me one more thing.

Is this the same man, my father, who taught me to ride a bicycle in the front yard? The same man who brought my first go-cart home and allowed me to totally ruin the grass in our back yard? The man whose strong arms would pick me up and toss me into the pool or the ocean? The man whose arms now are wasting away and cannot move unless someone moves them for him?

Is it the man laying in that bed the one who taught me as a child to always give a tithe back to God? The father who always waited on my brother, sister and me after Bible Study class by a wooden table outside the sanctuary so we could sit together because that is what families did in church. This is my father who tried his best to teach me the virtues of freshly polished shoes, but I still haven't quite caught on to that concept. The father who for many years worked six days a week to provide for our family, so that we could have food on our table, shoes on our feet and would make sure we always had all we needed . . . and then some. This is the father who believed in taking family vacations as long as any of us kids would go. The last vacation I had a chance to take with him and my mom was just a couple years ago and I find myself yearning for just one more trip that will now never happen.

My dad and I butted heads on more than a few occasions, but I never doubted his love for me and those occasions seem rather unimportant now. He loved my mother with a love that only God can give. He loved and supported my brother, sister and his grandchildren. And, oh, my gosh, how he loved his church! From the time I was a small boy until only five weeks ago, he was constantly at his church cutting grass, changing light bulbs, fixing anything that needed to be fixed. He wanted his house of worship to be beautiful for the God he served.

Now, we all wait. The nutrition and hydration tubes are out and we sit and reflect and laugh and cry (well, I am still working on that last one; it's something I'm not too good at). The healthcare workers at the hospice are truly God's angels here on earth in the love and care they show not only my dad, but also my mother. They are dedicated to making sure my dad's final days here on earth are peaceful, calm and comfortable. We have been told that most people in dad's condition may last three or four weeks, and we are ending week two. So, without some miraculous intervention, my dad will be with His Father God in a very short time. My family and I are sad and will grieve, but I know that someday we'll be together again. But, for now, we sit and wait and pray for an easy transition.

My mother's verse of strength that she has shared with us over the past month is found in Nahum 1:7. *"The Lord is good, a stronghold during the difficult times. He knows those who take refuge in Him."* I'm trying. I'm really trying to find that refuge and stay there.

My family and I appreciate your prayers and thoughts for my dad. God's will is taking place and He alone is giving us the 'peace that passes all understanding." I know that the person lying in front of me is only the personification of my father. My dad is alive in my heart and in everything I do and say. And, as for me, I'm heading out tomorrow to buy some shoe polish.

And for today my friends, with tears in my eyes and an ache in my heart, this has been the gospel according to Jimmy.

Free at Last!

Well, dear friends, my Dad is finally at peace and has gone to be with his God. It's 2 a.m. on Saturday morning here in Atlanta and he passed away around midnight at the hospice. They called our family to come in, so we drove over to say 'goodbye for now, but we'll see you soon" and I'm now back at home.

Dad had a peaceful, easy transition . . . . the kind we all hope for. He had been back in a coma for a couple days, gently asleep, and the nurse who was with him told us that he just simply took one more breath and transitioned quietly into physical death where God was waiting for Him with arms open wide with love.

I wish everyone could have known my dad. For better or worse, he is the one who helped form me into the man I am today. He would get all weird and stuff if any of us told him point-blank that we loved him, but I know he loved us because of the way he lived.

And for today my friends, this has been a long couple of months and I am tired and weary from the emotional upheavals, but it is a joyous gospel according to Jesus that assures me that my dad is already in His presence.

And for today, my friends, this has been the gospel according to Jimmy.

Life Through a Single Guy's Eyes

The Journey of Living Single

"Behold, I am with you and will keep you wherever you go, and will bring you back to this land; for I will not leave you until I have done what I have promised you." *(Genesis 28:15)*

"Not that I speak from want, for I have learned to be content in whatever circumstances I am." *(Philippians 4:11)*

I tend to get the question a lot, "How come a nice guy like you is still single?" "How has some young lady managed to let you escape?" Of course, on the inside they are thinking, "Sheesh, what is the matter with him that nobody would marry him?" "He looks nice, but he must have some type of 'condition'! I wonder if he has some abnormality underneath that hair?"

There was a time years ago that this would bother me and I would start to feel inferior, left out and like I had missed an important boat in the sea of life. However, as I've grown older both chronologically and spiritually, I have come to realize that being a single Christian has been a blessing that married people can never understand. When friends of mine were marrying and settling into that routine, I was able to spend more time with the student ministry at my church without having to worry about leaving my spouse alone too long. When these same friends were having children and raising them, I was able to spend time in mission endeavors without worrying about being gone from home for a week or two at a time. While my friends were having to maintain bedtime, homework, sports and cheerleading routines, I could stay on the phone with someone or have someone in my living room who just needed to talk to an adult about issues they were struggling with. And when these friends of mine would often call me with the news that they were separating and divorcing with the ensuing arrangements about children and finances, I was sorrowful, but thankful that I did not have to feel that kind of pain.

Do I want to marry someday? Sure. Do I enjoy the close relationship of a Christian lady who shares not only my faith and values, but my humor, happiness and sorrows? Sure. Have I met the "right one for me" yet? I don't think so, but sometimes I wonder if the one woman for me is living somewhere in Argentina and happened to miss the boat to the USA back in the 1970's. I've always just trusted God to use his divine sledgehammer to whack me into realization whenever she comes along.

My good buddy, Gabe, preached a sermon at church one night that was focused on encounters with God. In the story of Jacob leaving home in Genesis (verse above), Jacob made the self-discovery at Beth-el that God had been with him even when Jacob did not know it. Also, in the story of Moses at the burning bush, Gabe asked the question, "Had the bush been burning all along and Moses just never noticed it? Had the ground always been holy?" God promised Jacob that He would always be with him wherever he went and whatever he did. Not only that, God promised Jacob that He would never leave him until His purpose had been accomplished.

Now, how do I relate this to living a single life? Many people I know are consumed about the fact that they are not married, either by divorce, widowed, or never married. They feel alone, rejected and like they are not a complete person. They question why God has not given them a life mate when everyone else seems to have found theirs. They feel like they are not living a full life as God wants without a marriage and family to fulfill God's plan for their life. I would tend to disagree with this. To be honest, I would tend to disagree with this quite strongly.

Genesis 28:15 tells us that God is and will be with us always. Just because we don't recognize His presence in our single life, doesn't mean He isn't there all along. God was using Jacob and Moses all along, even though they did not recognize His presence the whole time. Once they recognized this, God was able to use them in great and mighty ways to accomplish His work. As single adults, we need to realize that God is very present in our lives and wants to use our single lifestyle for His glory and for His work and quit feeling so left out of His plan. You are in His plan, so just ask Him how you are to be used. Helping newly divorced or widowed people. Being supportive of single parents. Joining together in accountability with others to remain pure and socially in touch with God. Being a part of just a fun group of people who don't have to worry as much about curfews, homework and truant officers.

The apostle Paul was "content in whatever circumstances he found himself." One of those circumstances was being a single Christian guy and look how God used him. I do pray that God will bless me with a wife and family (even if blended) someday and I hope that it happens. But, you know, if it doesn't happen, then I'll be perfectly okay. I know that God will continue to use me in a ministry unique to my own gifts and talents (bizarre as they may seem at times.) More importantly, however, I just want to be used by God as an example that you can live a fun, exciting, fruitful and Godly life as a single Christian guy.

And for today my friends, this has been the gospel according to Jimmy.

A Dreaded Thing Appeared
In My Mailbox

A most dreaded thing appeared in my mailbox recently. A Jury Summons? An Income Tax audit? A subpoena to testify in a multiple murder and drug trial? My University diploma was being revoked due to unuse? No to all of the above. What did I see when I opened the mailbox? A big envelope with the horrid words "Welcome to the AARP".

Yep, Mr. Jimmy is getting older. I know because of the way I sometimes act and sometimes dress, it is hard to imagine . . . but, still it is true.

I instantly began having back pains, leg pains, blurred vision and a sudden craving for Metamucil and early bird dinner specials. All of a sudden, I felt the need to begin filing insurance papers in a logical manner like my parents do; the desire began to drive under the speed limit while craning my neck to see over the steering wheel and to call the children in my neighborhood 'whippersnappers'. I realized that before long I would be known as the strange old man down the street who walked his dog in his bedroom slippers and who had frogs for pets and named each one of them for Disney characters. Small children would avoid my house at Halloween.

After a period of time spent in self-indulgence and (almost) pity, I began to enter a period of self reflection. What have I accomplished in the past 50 years that is so great? This is what I came up with and hopefully as many of you face this same day in the coming years, you won't find it a tragedy, but instead a blessing.

God has blessed me with a good Christian family. My parents, my sister and my brother are all interesting characters in their own right, but we were raised with a love for the Lord and came into a knowledge of His saving grace as a natural part of our household teaching. I would not trade this for all the riches of the world.

God has not yet blessed me with a wife and children; however, He has given me the opportunity to have many children through the Student and Children's ministry at church. I have the chance to play with them, share my faith with them, make midnight Taco Bell runs with them, counsel them, sometimes burn illegal CD's with them, but always hopefully let them see that God is at work in my life and help them find their path into God's will for their lives. Plus, I get to go home at the end of the day to a nice quiet house and leave the tougher stuff to their parents.

God has blessed me in immeasurable ways through the Single Adult Ministry at my church. From the passing in the halls at church, to the putt-putt games, to the cookouts and firework watching, to the mountain hiking trips, to the Bible Studies where we learn more about each other, to the days of moving each other from place to place. I have friendships through YOU that I am thankful for each and every day.

I have been given a good career. I realize that I have been blessed with this job when so many folks around are not able to find work or are extremely dissatisfied with their place. My secular job has given me the chance to use my mind and my skills for business in a very intellectual and stimulating atmosphere.

Plus, I have been blessed with good health and well-being for these years. Oh, there have been scrapes and bruises (both physical and emotional), but with God's help and with the help of those around me, I have survived. Of course, someday my doctor hopes I will learn the meaning of "age appropriate behavior" and stay off the roller blades and rope courses. But, don't ever think that my life is any different than yours. We all have those days and weeks and seasons of trials, but with God's help we'll make it through.

All in all, my friends, it has been a good ride. A good set, so to speak in musical terms. I would not trade anything that I've experienced, the places I've been and the sights I've seen. Would I have done things differently? I don't think so. Because the man that I am today is a result of what I have been through, and I am quite pleased with whom I have become. And, as I always will tell you, I am nothing without God.

I want to encourage you to look forward to the day when you get your AARP card in the mail. It is a time to realize your place in life, to look back and reflect, but mostly to look forward to the person that God is continuing to form.

And for today my friends, this is the gospel according to Jimmy (the elderly one).

In the Sanctuary of my SUV

Hey boys and girls,

Quiz time. What would you say is one of the most common challenges facing Christian single adults? Not enough money to do what we want or need? Boredom? Not enough time in the day? Frustration raising children alone? Discouragement in not having a spouse? Tired of the same food groups of takeout, microwave and frozen? All of the above?

I'm certainly no expert on the matter (well, as a (cough)-something year old single guy, perhaps I am), but I seem to deal with the ongoing struggle to keep Christ first in my life. The lips might proclaim, "Yes, yes" but the heart is saying "Yeah, right . . . maybe tomorrow". Our jobs, family issues, reality television fixations and my quest for the perfect cup of coffee seem to take precedence over everything else. However, of one thing in life I am sure . . . . I do know that if Christ is the center of our hearts and of our homes and families then all the stuff in the first paragraph will take care of itself. Actually, the food part may stay, but that's okay because you still get to have your french fries and other comfort food.

The daily struggles don't disappear like we might want, but the burdens do lessen if you are walking through them with Christ and with the fellowship of other believers. The things that seem so important and so critical at times may pale in comparison to the importance of realizing the power of Christ in your life and in your heart.

You've heard me talk before about how important music is to me in my personal worship times. Last night on the way to church and then again this morning as I drove to work, I put in one of my favorite worship CDs. It has a lot of familiar praise and worship songs, but the Lord put just the right song on the play list. I had church on the way to work.

Friends . . . let me urge you today and everyday to take time to Know Jesus. Know the power of His love for you and your daily struggles. He has been there. He lived for thirty-three years as a single adult and He was fully human and faced so many of the same struggles which we do. Know Jesus in your heart, your life and continue knowing more and more about Him as the days go by. I promise that the burdens will not disappear, but they will be lightened and your walk will be straighter and more joyous.

And so for today my friends, this is the gospel according to Jimmy.

Well, Here We Go Again!

Many of those who know me think I am a 21st century Scrooge when it comes to the holiday season. Rarely do I do any decorating of the house for Christmas, I go to a very few holiday parties, and make all attempts to keep a low profile until Christmas is over. I will play holiday CD's in the car or in the office, but I can only take it for so long. Most of my shopping is done online and I avoid shopping malls and the mainstream stores like they have the plague. There are plenty of little mom and pop shops around the area and in the north Georgia mountains where very unique and personal gifts can be bought with little or no hassle of traffic and funds. Where possible, I prefer to make gifts and do the best I can to not compare prices of gifts I receive with those I give.

As I explain every year, I am not having a crisis of faith or anything at all. My belief in the birth of Christ is as strong and as important to me as ever. My celebration in the Joy of His birth grows with each year; however, my next statement is the one that most people can't quite grasp. Through the years, the church has ruined far too years of my personal Christmas joy and excitement. There have been too many musical performances that require too many extra evenings of rehearsal meaning time away from home and family. Too many 'expected to be at' parties and functions the other nights of the week meaning more time away from home. Far too many services and programs where attendance is almost required so that more time is taken away from my own time and space. For several years, the stress and anxiety surrounding the season caused me physical illness and ever since the year I was throwing up in the pastor's new rose bushes the week before Christmas, I have tried to not get caught into that trap again.

In my thoughts, the season of Advent and Christmas is a time when I want to spend time in personal and private reflection about my place in God's work. By focusing on writings by my favorite authors, devotionals and the Scriptures, I want to use this month to reflect upon the past year and where I need to be in the coming year in order to serve Him to my best ability. However, when my time has been demanded and stretched too far, my spiritual side begins to take on the same symptoms as my physical side. This is the reason why I now tend to try and withdraw from the entire hubbub facing us.

Being a single guy, I enjoy spending the season with family and some good friends. A good evening at home, fire in the fireplace, candles burning, music playing, catching up on emails with long ago friends, keeping close to my parents, brother and sister, and taking the time to write a personal note in a holiday card instead of the standard imprint for special people in my life. Add in a mug of hot cocoa, having some good friends in for chili or pot luck, and going caroling to those who are shut-in or in need of some holiday cheer. That's what the season is for; drawing closer to God, rejoicing in His love gift and sharing it simply and unselfishly with others. I think the church has lost sight of the simplicity of the season (in many cases) by trying to reach out to so many people that they wear out the few faithful ones.

So, don't think of me as Ebenezer, the Grinch or even Oscar the Grouch, because I am not. I am so blessed with my family, my church and a wonderful group of friends. But, as for me, over the next few weeks I just want to "Be Still and Know that He is God." I encourage you to do the same.

So for today my friends, this has been the gospel according to Jimmy.

Looking Back, Looking Forward

New Year's Eve . . . . Looking back, looking forward . . . . A time to start anew . . . . blah, blah, blah. Not being one to make resolutions in the past, I don't feel the inclination to do so tonight. Actually, I'm having a great New Year's Eve, sitting at home, washing clothes and enjoying the solitude of the house and the calming of my spirit as I instinctively look back at the past year.

Why do so many people wear themselves out trying to be all things to all people? We serve in so many areas at our churches, we have secular jobs to do which pay the bills most of the time, some folks have families and/or children to raise, in my case I am working on a graduate degree which takes up more time, and on and on and on. I hate to tell someone 'no' because I feel like I'm letting God down somehow to not be that "all things" person. Do I think that they will not like me any more because I say "Sorry, I can't do that" or that God will revoke my spiritual gifts license because I want to spend a night at home instead of being out and about? So, I will put on my 'all things to all people" t-shirt and gallop off on my spiritual high horse to keep everyone happy and joyful.

Is it only me? Are there others of you out there that have the "All Things" club T-shirt and membership ring? As for me, I am realizing that I can't be all things to all people if I have neglected my self and my own time with God. I have to grow in order to help others to grow. Sounds easy in theory, but it's quite tough to put into practice.

As I started out saying, I am not one to make resolutions, but I do try to make lifestyle changes. This year, I am going to try to please God by doing what He wants me to do and by being what He wants me to be. Same thing I said this time last year, and I did make some progress, but I will do more in the coming year. There are other avenues and paths for me to explore in His plan for my life and I am not content to travel the same paths as before. I will not be content to just settle for the status quo of my previous spiritual quest, but to continue in drawing closer to the personal God who has carried me safe for all these years, the bumpy ones as well as the smooth ones. I firmly believe with great excitement and anticipation that the same God who led Moses and Abraham, who inspired Paul and Peter, will be walking by my side tomorrow morning as I step outside into a new year. Wow! Ain't that a kick??

And for today my friends, this has been the gospel according to Jimmy.

Me and My Luggage

My friends hate to travel with me. Whether it is vacation, a weekend camping trip, an overnight hike or a musical tour, they hate to see my car pull into the driveway. Why is that? I am not one to travel lightly. Even if it is a weekend trip, there are always those circumstances for which I must plan.

You know, the 'what if I fall in the pool or lake more than once and need extra socks and pants' possibility. What if I find a good wireless connection for my laptop and I can get in some surf time? So, I usually end up with one bag full of my electronics (Laptop, iPod, Pocket PC, portable DVD player and various chargers and cables), then another bag full of twice as many clothes as I actually need, then another bag with the essentials of travel, like chocolate and potential water balloons.

The point is that I'm known for all the baggage I trundle along with as I travel the highways. Are you the same way? Regardless of how you pack for a trip, we all do have one thing in common and that is the unseen baggage that we carry. We have accumulated it from failed relationships, financial problems, abusive situations, employment problems, broken or dysfunctional families, lack of education and so many other areas far too numerous to name. It is much easier to leave a suitcase at home than it is to leave some of our internal baggage behind.

Now, before you get all excited about this being an expose' on my life I will just share that I have my own fair share of baggage. I've also learned that it does not matter what age we are, we can still add to the stack of luggage we carry and it gets heavier and heavier with each day unless we learn to deal with it. By this time in my life, I've got a trainload full. As a Christian, it is easy for me to say, 'Oh, just turn it all over to God and He'll take your cares away" (I Peter 5:7), but to be honest, sometimes that just doesn't cut it for me. My personality is one to take care of things myself and effect the changes I need to make.

One of my favorite vocalists and friends is Kirk Talley who wrote a song several years ago entitled "Past Your Past." In it he speaks of a young lady who was struggling with a lot of old baggage and could not put it behind her to begin living in today. The song goes on to encourage her (and us);

> *"You can get past your past. You can walk away from painful memories. Get past your past; you don't have to be alone. You can stand upon the Word of God; your yesterdays can be gone. Let Jesus bring you past your past and then you can go on."*

Music is the medium that speaks to my soul. Be it good jazz and blues, rock and roll, or contemporary Christian; music can stir me like no other vehicle. Each time I hear this song, I am reminded that I can put my baggage behind and move on into today. First I must ask God's forgiveness and then I have to forgive myself. It's hard, it's scary, it can be emotional and it may require accountability with others, but you can begin to leave your past behind, one tote bag at a time.

And for today my friends, this is the gospel according to Jimmy.

Murphy's Law—(a tongue in cheek story, but, sadly true)

What happens when a slightly obsessive-compulsive, a-retentive, borderline neurotic about organization guy hits the unexpected in his well-thought out schedules? On the outside all may seem well and calm, but on the inside a literal firestorm cauldron burns from the toes to the ears and consumes each body organ in between. Well, perhaps that was a tish dramatic, but we people do not usually like unexpected change. This was the case last Saturday.

My plans were made. I'd made them well in advance for Saturday. They were on my kitchen calendar, my office calendar, in my PDA, on my laptop calendar and sticky notes on the back door. There was a funeral to play for at 1:30 p.m., then pizzas to pick up at 5:30 p.m. for a party at 6:00 p.m. Simple. No problem. Everything was set and I was ready to face the day. Until . . . .

About 11:00 in the morning I had finished some work in the living room and went into the sun room to plug my laptop back in for charging. As I stepped into the kitchen, I noticed that my feet felt like they were covered with water. I glanced down and, lo and behold, they were!! The washer had picked that particular day to break down and flood my kitchen and sunroom. The water was laughingly (yes, I know it was laughing) edging toward the carpet in my living room. I let out a banshee shriek which sent Murphy scurrying under the bed, most of the local animals ran to the nearby wooded areas and parents grabbed their children off the sidewalks. Naturally, I grabbed towels and rugs and sheets and anything else that would absorb water and tossed them in effort to stop the flow. Murphy knew if he came out from under the bed, he would be flung in the river, too. After a few minutes, it occurred to me to turn off the machine and the water spigots.

With that done, I grabbed the wet-vac from a neighbor and began siphoning up the half-inch of water containing strange things with dark tendrils which had floated out from beneath the washer and dryer. When the vacuum suction started, Murphy abandoned my bed and went to the farthest room in the house and into the closet and found refuge under a stack of luggage. All I could see were two eyes and a snout quivering in the darkness. The wet-vac worked sufficiently and even got most of the water from the berber carpet in the solarium and in the el-cheapo carpet in the living room. Glancing at my watch, I realized I was supposed to be leaving for the funeral in about 20 minutes and still had not ordered the pizzas . . . . or taken a bath. So (and I'm embarrassed to admit this) I stuck my head under the kitchen spout to wet it enough to comb, grabbed some blue jeans and a polo shirt to wear (heck, what do they make choir robes for anyway?) and took off leaving Murphy wondering what had happened.

That one event threw off the rest of my day. A friend who called and heard the octave higher cadence of my voice volunteered to order the pizzas for me. After all the hubbub, the party that night was fun and a nice way to relax. But, my mind was still racing ahead to when I got home and had to start putting the furniture back into the kitchen, haul back in the areas rugs and doormats and put into the dryer BECAUSE I would never be able to go to sleep with the room in a mess like it was. Then there was the question of how I would wash the clothes I needed to wash and how much a new washer would cost (since this one was 28 years old and was time to replace anyway).

Fortunately, when I got home the floor was dry and most things could be put back into place. My plans were made and recorded on my calendars to shop for a new washer on Sunday afternoon. My hope was that it would be delivered on Monday so I could catch up on laundry Monday and Tuesday evenings after work. It succeeded. The plan went off without another hitch in the schedule and my world is once again a cozy place, except for Murphy who is still very hesitant to leave the safety of my bedroom. I tend to find humor in the fact that various aspects of the infamous Murphy's Law deal with expecting the unexpected and I also named my dog, Murphy. I should have suspected something. Plus, I am sure I gave God a good chuckle for the day . . . . probably a down right guffaw is closer to the truth.

And for today my friends, this has been the gospel according to Jimmy.

Lessons Learned from My Dog

Do you ever wonder what good you are possibly doing for the Kingdom of God? After all, your day is full of work, school, car pools, soccer, baseball, church, homework, taking care of children or aging parents, trying to have some type of social life, etc. So, then you fall into bed at the end of the day and (hopefully) at least say a prayer and read a scripture at some point, but, you are dead tired and wonder what difference you have made in someone's life for God today? And how you can possibly do any better?

My dog Murphy taught me the other day that even a little bit done can make a difference. My grass is brown. Brown all over. Dead looking brown. A field of dead hay would look as good as my front yard. Crayola doesn't even make a crayon color with this same ugly shade of brown. Get the point? When I was walking Murphy one afternoon I noticed that there were all these little holes about an inch or so in diameter all over the front yard. While I wondered what in the world (or what alien being) inhabited my yard, I happened to notice Murphy walking across the yard to do what, well, to do what dogs do when they are outside. At least what they do after they sniff every available leaf, cigarette butt, wet paper and dead bug.

Anyway, I noticed that his feet were making these little holes as he walked across the barren dead yard. If you know me much at all, you know how even a shiny object can fascinate me for hours, so I started to look down into these holes to see what was in there. You know what I saw? I saw more dead grass. But, deeper down in there I saw little blades of green new life. The grass was growing!! It was just covered up with old stuff and Murphy was uncovering it! Over the next day or two, I noticed that where all these little Murphy footprints were, that the new grass was growing quicker and higher than anywhere else in the yard. Of course, it looks rather strange now to have all these little pockets of green in the midst of the brown, but they are there. They just had a little help from my terrier.

Now, where I'm going with this? Murphy was just going about his normal daily routine, doing what dogs do. His feet are little and hardly make a dent, but it was enough to open up a small space to let the light in and start new growth.

We are the same way. If we go about our daily lives, doing what we normally do at work, school, home, wherever we are, AND if we do it as we live Christ's example here on earth . . . we make that little dent in someone's life, let some of God's light in and allow new life to begin to grow. We don't have to teach Sunday school, sing in the choir, lead a missions group, or any other church "things" to do the Kingdom work. We just have to live, as Christ wants us to live, meet people where they are, and make that little dent in their lives.

And for today my friends, this has been the gospel according to Jimmy.

Biting the Hand that Feeds You

As I moved the needle closer and closer my heart raced faster and faster. The unsuspecting patient had no idea that he was about to have a hypodermic syringe plunged into his neck in just a couple of seconds. He also had no clue that I had never done this before, but probably would never know that until the deed was done. My steady hand moved slowly to gather up a fold of skin in which to plunge the needle; deliberately and determinedly taking hold when all of a sudden the patient bounded up in a state of pure rage and grasped my hand with his teeth with all the fury which a fifteen pound terrier can muster.

Yes, I was attempting to give Murphy his first insulin shot. He was diagnosed several days ago and my lucky lot in life is to inject his neck with the insulin once a day. However, in the split second it took to bribe him to my lap with a treat, he turned from my always mild-mannered and loveable pet to the wild beast of the field that his ancestors were. As his head turned (much like Linda Blair in "The Exorcist") to engage my hand with his teeth, my survival mode kicked in to push him away with one hand, throw the needle across the room with the other hand and run shrieking as he gave chase. When the scene finally came to a calmer moment and I could come down from the top of my piano, I began to tell Murphy, "This is just supposed to help you! Why are you biting me? You have a disease and we need to do this in order to make you feel better, you ungrateful little dog! Why can't you understand that?"

Murphy has this way that he will cock his head to the side when I am on one of my tirades which makes it appear he is really listening, but then he will snort and turn around and trot off which lets me know how much he really cares. The same thing happened now. Head cocked, listen, snort and trot. I was beginning to feel some remorse and followed him with another treat, when he suddenly turned around and let out another primal snarl of warning to keep my distance . . . . leave the treat on the floor, but keep my distance. I obeyed.

So far, we have not come to an understanding about his method of treatment. Even though I know he needs this injection in order to have a better quality of life, Murphy simply will not allow it. His English pea sized brain can't comprehend this. He just knows that I am doing something which hurts him and he instinctively bites back.

Do we not do the same thing when God tries to keep us from harm? Do we not (figuratively) bite back when God tries to guide us in a way that we really don't think we want to go? All we know is that our "What I Want" world is being changed and the results seem rather painful and uncomfortable. And, to be honest, at first they are not always so pleasurable, however, if we have the faith in God which we should we know that following His plan of care will give us a better quality of life.

We pray "O Father, please show us which path you want for us to go," but when He does, and we don't really like the route, we rebel. We pray "God, please help me to be a stronger witness for you," but when He attempts to teach us strength through obstacles and personalities, we run whimpering back to our safe little world.

Even though he is a very intelligent dog, Murphy does not have the reasoning ability that humans do. He only knows that I feed him, play with him and will always take care of him. That belief was threatened, so he responded with his inbred canine nature. We have the ability to know that God loves and cares for us and would never put us in a position which we could not handle (depending on His strength and help), yet we respond all too often with our human nature of self desires.

Someday, hopefully, Murphy will trust me enough to give him the medicine he needs to bring him back to good health and a right relationship with his own body. He cannot stay at this point for long or his health will deteriorate and he will die. If we do not allow God to inject us with stronger faith and life experiences, we will grow stagnant and become less useful disciples. Trust the hand that feeds you!

And for today my friends, this is the gospel according to Jimmy.

The Rock and a Hard Place

I'm kinda bummed. After my earlier writing about Murphy and the diabetes and the shots, I felt quite confident in my ability to make it work tonight. He and I both had a couple calm days and had seemed less aggressive when I would pet him and play with his fur and skin where I would need to give a shot. So, tonight, I once again got the needle ready, gave Murphy his supper and he gobbled it down, drank some water then promptly hopped up on my lap. However, even with my calm talking and letting him lick my hand and arm, as soon as I made a move toward his head or back, the snarls and teeth came out. After several attempts, I finally discarded the hypodermic and gave up once again.

I cannot justify the restraining and pure anger that would be created in my fourteen-year old dog every day for the rest of his life. Plus, being single, I don't have someone readily available in the evenings to help me hold, muzzle and restrain him. And, even if I were able to give him a shot tonight, there is certainly no guarantee that I could pull it off again for several days.

He is now lying on the sofa watching me with still suspicious eyes. My heart hurts because I feel like I am signing an early death warrant for my good friend for many years. He has Cushing's disease which has enough issues, but is being treated by a pill (which he is fine with taking), he also has high thyroid levels, but is also taking a pill for that, which seems to be working.

I know Murphy well enough to see that he doesn't feel well and I just can't bring myself to agitate and anger him more on a daily basis with this shot. It is kind of a Catch-22 because he would probably feel better if he could get the shots, but I just can't do them. I cannot put him into a headlock and restrain him on the floor or in a holder for these shots every day. He would hate me. I can't afford to take him to one of the local PetStores or to the vet every day for the rest of his life, so I am torn over what to do.

If he were human, I would probably be arrested for considering withholding medication which he needs, but he isn't human, he is just a dog. But, he is my dog, my pet, and I only want him to be happy and live peacefully as long as he can and a daily fight with me over a shot isn't very peaceful. I realize that there is war, crime, abuse, hunger and so many things in the world of greater impact, but this is what consumes my mind now.

And for today my friends, with a heavy heart, this has been the gospel according to Jimmy.

A Day of Loss

"A good man cares for the life of his animals." (Proverbs 12:10 ESV)

As you know, many of the ideas and inspirations for articles come from my dog, Murphy. It is amazing how watching a small dog can teach so many lessons that I can apply to my life. He had no formal training, i.e., he knew a lot of words and commands, just not what they meant. I could say "Sit" and he might sit, but it was just as likely that he would lick my ankle. "Stay" might as well mean that there was a treat hidden in the grass under the tree for all the good it did. But, let me say the word 'ball' and he would immediately perk his ears up and head for the backyard because he knew a time of throw and catch was coming. Oddly enough, he never quite understood the word "outside," but if I said "It is 10:00, Murphy," he would head to the back door. It could be any time at all, but 10:00 was his key word for a bathroom trip. Like I said, he isn't the smartest dog in the world, but he taught me a lot through our adventures.

After fourteen years, my best friend and companion, Murphy, has passed away. He had been diagnosed with Cushing's disease and most recently with diabetes and his little terrier body just couldn't handle both of them. He has been with me through the best of times and the worst of times and was always waiting at the back door with a wagging tail and a licking tongue to welcome me home. During the bad times, he would curl up next to me on the bed or the sofa and take care of me as only a dog can. Every so often, he would turn his head to look at me and then give a little lick to let me know he was there. He had been feeling so bad for several days, was but never in any pain or suffering. That last night, I could sense that his time was short and I told him that it was okay. He could let go and that I would miss him, but I would be okay. Sometime, during the night, Murphy left my world peacefully in his sleep. There is a large hole now that is filled with pain and sorrow, but I'll be fine in time. There's something special about your first dog and Murphy was certainly something special. He taught me about unconditional love when I needed to learn it. He gave me many insights to life that I needed to learn.

I know it is not theologically sound, but, I would like to believe that Murphy and all family pets everywhere that have gone on before him are someplace nice, sunny and full of treats, water and love. They are no longer old or sick, but just like we remember them best; running through the grass in the sun, chasing things underneath your feet while you try to cook a meal and pushing your newspaper out of the way so they can curl up on your lap.

As for me, it has been a tough couple weeks now and even though I still hurt inside and miss Murphy, the healing has begun. My niece is making a Murphy Scrapbook for me which will be a treasured possession. I wonder if my new aquarium will provide as many entertaining stories . . . . you never know.

I'll never forget you, Murphy-dog. You were the best.

The Hound Of Heaven

One of the predominant traits of a dog like Murphy is what is sometimes called the "tenaciousness of a terrier." Even as the smallest puppy, he would show me a stubborn streak both in playing and in training. I quickly learned that this was to be a characteristic that would dominate most, if not all, of our lives together. We would play tug of war and that little beast had no hesitation to do his best to haul me across the room and would not give up until I either let him drag me or I simply let go. Or, we would be outside for a walk and there might be a new fallen leaf which he had not smelled. Knowing that he would stand there and sniff for an hour, usually I would haul him back inside, however the next time we left the house, he would head right to that leaf for his smelling time.

Once Murphy set his mind to something, he would not be deterred. Once, a lizard got into the house and I was able to capture it safe and sound under an empty butter tub and Murphy was dead set and determined to dig through me, my legs, the broom, a kitchen table and the butter tub to see that lizard. Of course, I released the lizard back out the door and having seen that, Murphy would prowl the yard for days knowing that 'his' lizard was out there just waiting to be smelled.

Murphy was tenacious, he would not give up if he wanted something and he would keep after a project (like digging a hole in the yard right in the middle of my best centipede) until he was completed to his satisfaction. God has often been referred to as 'the Hound of Heaven." After observing and learning from Murphy, I think I finally understand what that statement means.

God is tenacious. He will not give up on any of us. No matter how hard I play tug of war with God over decisions and circumstances, He will not let go of His side of the rope. I may let go of my end and walk off, but God will throw that rope back in my path at some point and the game will begin again. I have learned through many days and nights that His love is the most stubborn thing in creation. It never fails, it never gives up, it never runs out. That is a quality far beyond human comprehension.

Am I the only one who seems to try and divert God's attention away from things? He may want me to be focusing on a certain devotional, sermon topic, career decision; however, often I will begin to tell God "Oh, well, yeah . . . I see that, but look at what I can do over here! Don't you remember when I spent part of a summer doing mission work in New York?" And the whole time, He waits for my diversion tactics to wind down, then he gently (sometimes not so gently) points my vision back to the present and what He is wanting now. Then, there are the occasions that I try to convince God of the path I should be going and why He should open those doors. Needless to say, that technique doesn't always work and I should have learned that lesson long ago.

This may not be the most doctrinal or theologically sound statement, but I think God must surely be amused at my efforts sometimes. I have always felt God as such a personal part of my life that I tend to think of Him in an almost familiar sense at times. I am totally convinced of His love for me and that He continues to guide me in my everyday life. I love Him with all my being and we have been like best friends all my life. Even when I rebel and argue and attempt to go my own way, it is such a comfort to know that my God is there waiting and loving me all the time.

A friend told me in a recent email after Murphy passed away that it is no coincidence that God is Dog spelled backwards. I think that is why Murphy tried so hard in his time with me to get me to learn things that I needed to learn about life, love and God. Friends . . . don't forget how much God loves each of you, regardless of your acknowledgement of Him or not. He is the tenacious "Terrier of Heaven" and His love is always waiting for you when you finally decide to come home to Him. And, believe me, His welcome beats a wet lick on the nose any day.

So for today my friends, this is the gospel according to Jimmy.

My House Speaks

"As for me and my house, we will serve the Lord." (Joshua 24:15)

If you look around my house, you'll find the above verse in several places. It's above the door from the kitchen to the sunroom, on a coffee mug, on a picture hanging in my office and also used as part of my email signature. The verse has always been a powerful reminder from Joshua to the nation of Israel that he and his family were choosing that day to serve Jehovah God instead of the pagan gods of the land.

The other day I was at work, washing out the coffeepot to get ready for the next morning, when the thought hit me out of the blue. "How does my house serve the Lord?" Sure, I do the best I can to serve the Lord each day by my actions, but how does my house serve the Lord? I am a single guy, so there is no immediate wife or kids there to lead in the Lord's way and to the best of my knowledge my house doesn't have the ability to witness to others . . . or does it?

If you come in my home, you'll always find a Bible and several Christian books sitting on the coffee table or the end tables. You'll find pictures of family and friends from church doing church things. There are various symbols of my faith and walk with Christ on walls, tables and on bookshelves. However, it struck me like a bolt of lightning that often a Bible or commentary is laying on top of the television where I might be watching a program or movie that isn't the most appropriate for a Christian. I might be writing an article or working on a Bible Study lesson while listening to a radio station or CD that isn't offering the most Christ-like values. On the same bookshelves where I keep different translations of the Scriptures and seminary course books, you could find some novels that are not the most edifying for a Christian to be reading. You won't find my refrigerator full of alcoholic beverages or any cigarettes and drugs in my cabinets, but you will find food and snacks that tempt me to not keep my body as the temple of God in the best of physical shape and abilities. At one time I even realized that playing video games was taking far too much of my time that should be spent doing productive work for God, so I got rid of my games and player to avoid the temptation.

Are you catching my point? It's now difficult for me to proudly proclaim, *"As for me and my house, we serve the Lord."* Obviously, I'll be doing some housecleaning over the next few weeks as I try to bring my whole being and whole house more into line with God. In the workplace, I do not allow inconsistencies to take place in areas under my responsibility. Why is my home any different? This is the place where I am; well, at home. Home. There's no place like home. A place of rest. A place of refuge. Home is the place where I should be able to meet God the easiest of any other place.

My only desire in life is to serve God and to point others to Him. I have traveled a number of summers doing mission and evangelism work around the United States; yet here at home, in my own house, I have been confronted with the fact that I need to get my own act together before I can help others.

And so for today my friends, this has been the gospel according to Jimmy.

Valentine's Day and the Single Guy

Valentine's Day and the Single guy. Does that sound like an oxymoron to you? Or does it sound like the title to one of the old "Love American Style" shows (yeah, now THAT really shows my age)? I mean, the national day of love, flowers and candy for your sweetie pie, all the e-card sites being slow as molasses because of the cards being sent, all the jewelry and dinners and red satiny things that I can't believe anyone would really wear at anytime of their life. I noticed at the grocery store today how many guys were buying the last of the scraggly little roses with slightly brown tinted baby's breath at 6 p.m. on the way home because they didn't plan ahead. Almost like Christmas, the pressure to do and/or buy just the right thing seems to be almost paramount to the reason for the day.

Now, I realize I don't have a lot of room to talk, but it seems to me that you folks should be letting your spouses or loved ones know all year long how much you love and care for them. It should not come down to just one day when you have to worry about buying the right candy or the right flowers or go to the right restaurant. Love should be a constant thing. And I do see that in many of my married friends. For some, it's obvious that they are in a love relationship with each other and with God because it shows in their lives and in their families.

Isn't it a good thing that God doesn't wait for February 14 each year to demonstrate His love toward us? Aren't we glad that He gave us the best love gift available? I am glad that in the love relationship with God, I don't have to worry about Him leaving me for another person or worry about making Him mad and being left alone. The ultimate Valentine giver will *"never leave us or forsake us" (Hebrews 13:5)*.

As the poster boy for the single life, I know that that the love of God is my greatest comfort. Sure, it may not keep my feet warm at night, but His Love does keep my heart warm 24/7. Like the apostle Paul, I have learned to be content with the conditions of my life. In fact, I am more than content because God has given me a family, friends and a church that enriches me at every thought. And I am able to do much in ways of ministry because I am single at this time and having more time available to give.

"For God loved the world so very much, that He gave up His only Son so that whoever believes in Him will not die spiritually, but enjoy an everlasting life." (John 3:16).

And for today my friends, this is the gospel according to Jimmy.

Why Not Me?

$\mathbf{A}$ twelve-year old boy sat in his room one Saturday night unable to concentrate on the television, a book or anything. All he kept asking was "Why not me, God? Why not me? I should have been in the car with them, but at the last minute the plans changed. If I had been in there would I have been killed? Would I be crippled? Would my best friend not have died?"

Perhaps because of his infancy in Christ, the boy didn't hear God's answer. All he felt was loneliness and that funny ache in his heart and stomach. The funeral was held the next day and the boy watched as the friend he had played with, confided with, argued with, but always considered his best friend was eulogized. He watched as they lowered his casket into the ground. "I don't understand, God. Why is he dead? He was just twelve years old and I didn't think twelve year old kids could die. Why can't he come over to my house this week like he always does? Why am I still alive and unhurt?"

The boy grew to be a man and at times would occasionally forget about his best friend from childhood, but when he did remember, the question was still there . . . . unanswered . . . . "Why not me, God? Why not me?"

One day, totally unexpectedly, God answered the boy who was now a man. During a sermon one Sunday, the Pastor quoted a verse from Jeremiah 29:11, *"For I know the plans that I have for you," declares the Lord, "plans for welfare and not for calamity and to give you a future and a hope."*

And then later, the boy heard the verse that would become the theme-verse for his life. *"Who knows but for such a time as this that you have been placed in this position?"* (Esther 4:14)

The man realized that perhaps God wanted him to be here to serve Him by using a gift of music that had been given him, to serve Him with the BSU, NAMB and local churches in mission trips to Charleston, New York City, Washington DC, St Simons Island and other places by sharing the message of "God Loves You and So Do I." Or, to serve Him in trying to be a positive adult leader and friend to teenagers and younger adults looking for their own answers to their walk with God. Perhaps God wanted the man to stay so that he could learn how to minister through church recreation and sports so that many people would come to a church and know the love of God through these avenues. He may have wanted him to be here for the strength and spiritual maturity he has gained from his friends.

The answer is still being answered for this boy who is now a man. How do I know? As I'm sure you've guessed by now, the boy, the man, is me. And the question is continually being answered by God as I try to stay receptive to His leading me in the paths that He wants. A change is coming in my life. I know this with all certainty because I have felt the leading before. A new avenue of ministry, perhaps? I don't know and I don't worry about it because the boy who cried out to God many years ago, now has the answer.

"You are are still here, my son, because I needed you here. Because you were here, other people have been blessed whether by your words or your actions and you may never have known about it. Just know that I have plans for you and will watch after you as you follow in the path I have for you. Above all, know that I love you and I love your friend who is now with me."

Let me encourage any of you reading this that God has you in His plan, whether you realize it or not. He loves you and he will use you in any place that you happen to be. Just stay faithful and strong and seek His way.

And for today my friends, this has been the gospel according to Jimmy.

What Does Your Coffee Table Say?

If someone came into your house and looked around your house at the books lying around, what perception would they have of you? Last night, I was sitting on my sofa watching television and propped my feet up on my coffee table. Everytime I do that, there is always a stack of books and papers that I will push out of the way and last night, I pushed a bit too much and they fell on the floor. Grumbling, I got up to pick them up and stack them again and began to notice that the seven books were: two Bibles (The Message and a NASB version), The Purpose Driven Life, Encountering God (daily devotions by Henry Blackaby), The Five Love Languages for Single Adults (for a discipleship class I'm teaching), The Ragamuffin Gospel, and Twelve Ordinary Men (a study of the disciples).

As I noticed the titles, I thought to myself, "Wow, if someone looks at this stack, they would think I am quite the spiritual guy!". That thought amuses me, not because I don't have a degree of spirituality about me, because I do . . . but, I would also have to admit that I really enjoy reading some of the fluff and mindless novels more than the theological ones. Perhaps that is because I am currently in Seminary and having to read theological books and papers all the time and when I get a break, I want to read something that doesn't require a lot of soul-searching and/or thought. If you looked in my bookbag, you would find a Patricia Cornwell novel and a Dan Balducci bestseller. On the table by my bed is The DaVinci Code, My Descent Into Death and the latest Harry Potter (while anxiously awaiting the next edition in June). Basically, when it comes to books and to music, I have no taste. I will read just about anything and everything and will listen to classical, hard rock, some rap, Christian praise and worship, southern gospel and country music.

My overall life is about the same, quite eclectic and no particular rhyme or reason. I am a quite good musician with very little musical training. I have worked in accounting for 26 years having never taken an accounting class ever and failed both high school and college algebra because mathematics doesn't make sense to me. I can converse with passable Spanish, German and American Sign Language, but only because during periods of boredom I would buy a book and tape at the bookstore. I'm pretty stinky at golf, but I used to be really bad until my friend, Joe, had extreme patience and helped me (because I was embarrassing him on the course). My humor is odd and quirky, often irreverent and sometimes not even understood. Somedays I will dress like a twenty-something, other days I can wear a tuxedo and pass for quite a dapper 50 year old man. However, my general mood and attitude is fairly constant and consistent unless you know the right buttons to push and I can snap like a rubber band.

I guess my point is that I might tend to be a hard person to read and get to know, or as we say here in the South, a tish eccentric. But, the one thing I hope is always clear and seen is my walk with my God. He is my driving force, my reason for getting out of bed in the mornings and what keeps me from whirling out of control on some of the crazy days. He is my strength in the really weak times and my protection when the storms of life are crumbling my foundations. He is my laughter, my joy, my humor, and even at the core of my eccentricities. He is my God and I am His. I have seen Him do miraculous things in the lives of my friends and family. I have felt His love surround and forgive me even when I deserved it the least. When I am angry with Him, He can handle it and gently leads me back to His side.

If you look around my house, you'll see a guy with a lot of different tastes and styles, but hopefully, you'll notice the coffee table first because that is where I do most of my work and writing. The coffee table is in the center of my living room which is the most important room in my house; the room of comfort, relaxation and where I am just being me. And my God is at the center of my life, where I am comfortable, relaxed and He knows the real me.

What does your coffee table say about you?

And for today my friends, this has been the gospel according to Jimmy.

Being a Man of God

Many times I tend to forget my chronological age (which is that of a middle-aged adult) and get caught up more into my attitudinal age (which is somewhere between sixteen and twenty one). Or, at least until I try roller blading, ropes courses, wrestling and other age-inappropriate behavior and end up in the emergency room with sprained and swollen ankles and wrists. And then at times, I will become more reflective, almost to the point of becoming maudlin, about my place in life and what I have done and what I want to accomplish in the years ahead.

What is involved in being a Man of God? Is it as easy as my great grandfather used to tell me? "I don't drink and I don't chew and I don't go with girls who do!". Does it mean to walk around with my big black reference Bible quoting scriptures verses about God's Law to anyone who will listen? Or, is it a little more involved?

Being a single guy, I sometimes feel that I have more to prove to those around me about my spiritual walk as a Man of God. After all, I have no wife to be my helper and partner in ministry and no children to be my crowning accomplishment and to train up in the ways of God. Not that I haven't prayed for a wife and family, but God just hasn't determined the time to be right and I'm quite okay with the single life. In actuality, though, how does that prevent me from being a Man of God? The scripture tells us that the man should be the head of the house, to love his wife as Christ loves the Church and to train up his children in the ways of the Lord. When Murphy was alive, I never could convince him to wear his little coat and tie and come to church with me, so that part may be moot. He was not particularly submissive to me, so I guess I struck out on that count, also. Does that mean I am not a Man of God?

I look around me at men in my church that I would consider Men of God, many of them younger than I am. Strong men of the faith, never ashamed to share their testimony, always greeting one another with a smile and a firm handshake or a hug, working with children in Bible Study, mission projects and other areas of ministry. I see men not afraid to weep during times of prayer and praise and always stand ready if the pastor asks for someone to come counsel with someone at the altar. These men are the first to step forward if a need is present and none of them care about recognition for their service.

Being born and raised in the South, there are two words that every southern man is raised to consider most important in their way of life: Honor and Integrity. Without these qualities you are not considered a true gentleman. As a Man of God, we are also given instructions on how to live. As Micah tells us, *"He hath shewed thee, O man, what is good; and what doth the LORD require of thee, but to do justly, and to love mercy, and to walk humbly with thy God?* "(*Micah 6:8*). I don't know about you, but I also see undercurrents of honor and integrity included in those words. The men in my church whom I look up to and consider mentors have these qualities. However, most importantly, when they make a mistake and fall short, they are the first to admit their shortcoming and ask forgiveness at both the altar of their fellowman and the altar of God. Humility, humbleness, honor.

My involvement with the teenagers at my church gives me satisfaction like none other. The fun, the laughs and the pranks will be unforgettable (even though our student pastor puts me on probation at least once a year for my involvement with the pranks). I also find it satisfying when one of the students comes to me with questions about their faith, questions about their family relationships, questions about their sexual purity as a Christian young man, questions about their careers, questions about whom to date and other important issues to them. I don't have all the answers, but I look with them into the scriptures and share things that God has taught me and led me to understand in hopes that it will help them in their paths. And then when I get that quick punch in the stomach (which is teenspeak for a hug), and I see a tear in their eyes and a relaxed smile on their face, I know that God is with them and my love for them grows. I learned when I was a Minister of Youth to "always take puppy love seriously because it is so serious to the puppies." Some of the things they come to me and other adults to discuss may seem somewhat unimportant, but it is important to them and they should be treated with respect and honor. (Of course, I also learned to not let sixty teenagers loose in Times Square and then take off running down 42nd street waving a clear plastic bag with over $800 in cash inside trying to make it to the Circle Line tour boat on time, but that's another story for another time.)

So, back to the original question. How can we be Men of God? Just do it. Love others, treat them with honor and respect, be an example to your family and to those around you, be a leader in your home, church, job and community, ask God each and every day to use you as His vessel here on earth so that others can see Jesus in you and don't be afraid to share the love of God when the situations arise.

Even though I might be a bit quirky at times, I am a Man of God. Let me encourage you other guys to find your place in God's work as Men of God, standing firm and strong for future generations.

And for today my friends, this has been the gospel according to Jimmy.

Afterword

This whole process has been a new experience for me and I am humbled that people may actually read these words and receive some encouragement or inspiration, have a laugh or even shed a tear. During the past couple of years as I began to write articles and journals from my daily walk, I have been amazed at what I have learned about God's plan for my life.

I give Him all the credit and honor for these words. His faithfulness to me through my life and the lives of my family and friends gave me the inspiration to see how He works in the most marvelous (and, yes, sometimes humorous) ways.

Thank you for buying this book and sharing a bit of my life and walk with God. My hope is that perhaps one story or one instance in *Being God's* will give you a moment of hope to know that God loves you and is concerned about every aspect of your life; no matter how trivial it seems to be.

Until we meet again, this has been the gospel according to Jimmy.

Jimmy Cochran
Stockbridge, Georgia
2006